"Inside these pages are the natural emotions and authentic expressions of fear and frustration experienced by caregivers. Anyone (men and women) who has endured the stresses of sickness, disease, or death of a loved one can relate to these emotions. With wisdom and authenticity, these authors offer calming words of hope, patience, and understanding. The commitment, perseverance, tenacity, and harmony with God will encourage your heart and help you make it through trying times. You'll find your faith increasing, your sense of humor bubbling, your hard days shorter, your frightening times peaceful as you live *through* the middle of God's faithfulness to you."
—Thelma Wells, speaker and author, A Woman of God Ministries

"The most practical book I've ever read, for the most neglected person I know—the family caregiver. Written by four women who've been there, *Strength for the Journey* chronicles such daily trials as fear, anger, loneliness, exhaustion, and guilt with candor, warmth, and, above all, answers that work." —Elizabeth Sherrill, contributing editor, *Guideposts,* author of *Journey into Rest*

"These authors know that life as a caregiver is tough. They also know the One who can make us strong. I highly recommend this book to those who need help for their journey." —Sharon Fish, author of *Alzheimer's: Caring for Your Loved One, Caring for Yourself*

"With uncommon candor and unsurpassed compassion, all of these remarkable women pour out their pain, joy, sorrow, guilt, and struggles in order to let other caregivers know, 'you are not alone.' Demonstrating the same faith-filled response they gave to those they were called to care for, the authors give both uplifting spiritual advice and down-to-earth practical suggestions for dealing with some of life's most difficult situations. If you or someone you know is involved in caregiving, this is one book to keep close at hand—and close to the heart." —Woodeene Koenig Bricker, editor, *Catholic Parent*

Strength
for the
Journey

Elsie J. Larson, Deborah Hedstrom,
Marcia A. Mitchell, and Lucibel Van Atta

HAROLD
SHAW
PUBLISHERS

Wheaton, Illinois

ISBN 0-87788-790-X.

Cover design by David LaPlaca and Thomas Leo
Interior design by Thomas Leo

Library of Congress Cataloging-in-Publication Data
Strength for the journey : encouragement for caregivers / Elsie Larson . . . [et al.].
    p. cm.
    ISBN 0-87788-790-X (pbk.)
     1. Caregivers Prayer-books and devotions—English.   2. Caregivers—Religious Life.
I. Larson, Elsie J.
BV4910.9.S77   1999
242'.68—dc21
                                     99-19006
                                      CIP

04 03 02 01 00 99
10 9 8 7 6 5 4 3 2 1

Dedication

To Mr. and Mrs. C. W. Hedstrom, who helped me be a caregiver to their son.
—*Debbie Hedstrom*

To my sisters Dorothy Kilber, Edith Bates, and Alice Parker, my fellow caregivers for our mom and dad.
—*Elsie Larson*

Lovingly, to those fellow caregivers who helped me handle "one more day" and gave me encouragement to write for them.
—*Marcia A. Mitchell*

To Susan—my daughter, my friend—who has been a loving caregiver to me and to many others.
—*Lucibel Van Atta*

Contents

Acknowledgments

I want to acknowledge my grown children—Jim, Jerry, Julie, and Janet—who have remembered my goodness and forgotten my failings.
—*Debbie Hedstrom*

A special thank you to my fellow authors of this book—Debbie, Marcia, and Lucibel—for sharing my dream for this book and for working so faithfully to complete it, despite painfully difficult times in their own schedules and lives.
—*Elsie Larson*

Thanks to our editors Joan Guest and Elisa Fryling and Harold Shaw Publishers for believing in this book. Thanks also to my critique group—Vi, Sam, Pat, Debbie, Charlotte, Cathy, and Connie—for their wonderful insight and help with these devotions.
—*Marcia A. Mitchell*

Special thanks to Elsie Larson, who patiently encouraged me to write these devotions in the midst of an incredibly difficult time of my life. Her organizational skills are matched only by her consistent Christian values. What a blessing to share in a critique group with her these many years!
—*Lucibel Van Atta*

Preface

As caregivers we have found the Lord's words to the Philadelphian church to be true today. "I know your deeds. See, I have placed before you an open door that no one can shut. I know that you have little strength, yet you have kept my word and have not denied my name. . . . Since you have kept my command to endure patiently, I will also keep you" (Rev. 3:8-10).

We know that no matter how things may look from our viewpoint, God truly does love our loved ones, and us, more than we can love each other. He does work all things together for good when we love him. He places before us open doors of hope.

Before we relate our caregiving experiences of hope, we'd like to give you more information about ourselves and our families.

Debbie Hedstrom cared for her husband, Art, at home during the last four months of his life while he battled cancer. She knows what it is like to have a hospital bed and IV tubes be the center of a home. Her four children were between the ages of eight and twelve during this time. She did not re-marry, and she understands the stresses a single parent faces raising adolescents.

While two of her three children were teenagers, Elsie Larson, with her three sisters, cared for her father and then her mother in her parents' home for a total of eleven years. During that time Elsie also became surrogate mother for two preschool grandchildren for eighteen months. Additionally, her husband has been frequently disabled with clinical depression.

After twelve years as a single mother, Marcia Mitchell married a widower with three children. She lost the companionship of her husband when he was diagnosed with Alzheimer's disease at the age of forty-one—on their ninth wedding anniversary. Marcia cared for Lee at home for seven years before he went into a nursing home, at which point she finished raising their six children alone. Two of her children were special needs adoptees—a daughter with Fetal Alcohol Syndrome and a son who had spent his first six years in foster homes and never had bonded to a mother.

Lucibel Van Atta faced the shock of almost losing her husband to a massive stroke soon after the couple went to the mission field. It had been their dream to work and teach in the Philippines when Bob retired from teaching at Portland State University. Now he is partially disabled, and she is his "partial" caregiver. Lucibel was also surrogate mom and caregiver to fourteen international high school and college students for more than a decade.

The challenge of being caregivers has pulled us closer to God. As we have leaned on him, he has strengthened us. It is our prayer that our experiences will encourage you on your caregiving journey as you draw on God's strength and receive his hope.

Debbie Hedstrom, Elsie Larson, Marcia A. Mitchell, Lucibel Van Atta

Not If, But When

Becoming an instant caregiver in a foreign country, the Philippines, brought me a sense of inadequacy that I had never experienced before. Totally overwhelmed by Bob's stroke, I remember crying out to God asking *How are we going to get through this?* Although I didn't doubt God's ability to cover any situation, I knew myself, and I foolishly wondered how I could be adequate.

Eventually, however, I came to realize the truth of this Bulgarian proverb: God promises a safe landing, but not a calm passage.

I only asked God to give me the spiritual strength to hold on during that crisis, and to stay close to us. The Lord's presence became as real as the humid, polluted air outside those Manila hospital walls, and my faith was forged into an indestructible shield. Whenever inadequacy's inner voice overwhelmed me, God reminded me that since he knit me together while I was still in my mother's womb, it would not be a difficult thing for him to reweave my unraveled mind and emotions.

During that month of hospital experiences, the endearing words of Isaiah 43:2-3 resonated in the corners of my numbed mind:

> When you pass through the waters, I will be with you; and when you pass through the rivers, they will not sweep over you. When you walk through the fire, you will not be burned; the flames will not set you ablaze. For I am the LORD, your God.

I was grateful that Isaiah used words such as *when you pass through,* not *if you make it through.* He told us specifically what Jehovah would do for us.

"Cast your cares on the Lord and he will sustain you; he will never let the righteous fall" (Ps. 55:22).

Thanks, Lord, that you understand how tenaciously we caregivers hang on to the distinctives of your promises—even little words such as *if* and *when*. In the midst of rough times we look forward to that safe landing you have provided, to the time when we will be with you in heaven. (LDV)

Beyond My Fears

Cancer, bulimia, stroke, Downs Syndrome, Alzheimer's—each is simply a medical term until spoken by a doctor about someone we love. From the moment we hear "I'm sorry; the test shows your husband (or child or parent) has _____," the word becomes the catalyst for a hundred fears. Our minds race with the worries while our emotions are torn apart or shocked into a frozen unreality.

I could push aside my fears when I was with my husband, Art. It helped to be close to him, doing little things, or simply sitting by his hospital bed. But when the hum of my van engine kept me company on the drive home, when my four children chattered around the missing place setting at the dinner table, and when I stared into the darkness from my half-empty bed, that's when fears crowded my mind. Over and over I tried to sort out all that went with Art's cancer and the surgery it required. I struggled to foresee its effect on him, our closeness, our children, and our finances. Everything I imagined frightened me and overran the lonely moments of my days. I slept little and cried a lot.

Somehow I kept reading my Bible through my fear. I'd started the book of Isaiah right before Art's diagnosis and had just kept going, though few of the prophet's words produced coherent thoughts in my anxious mind. The morning I turned to chapter 8, however, something happened. I was reading as usual, barely registering the words as I battled my fears. *Will Art pull away from me? What if he dies? How can I ever be a single mom?*

Amid my turmoil, I saw the word *fear* on the Bible page. It stopped me. I wanted to know what was being said about the very thing I was struggling with. "Sanctify the LORD of hosts himself; and let him be your fear, and let him be your dread. And he shall be for a sanctuary" (Isa. 8: 13-14, KJV).

Oh, how I wanted God to be my sanctuary! But first I had to set him apart as the controller of my circumstances and as the one to be feared. Only then could my lie-awake, tearful fears become a keep-me-pleasing-you fear.

I memorized the verse. I needed its assurance to quiet my mind. I needed its truth to battle new fears yet to come. And I needed its promise when what I had feared became reality.

"Oh, how great is your goodness, which you have laid up for those who fear you, which you have prepared for those who trust in you in the presence of the sons of men!" (Ps. 31:19, NKJV).

Lord, fear is so real. Transform it as only you can—from fear of circumstances to fear of you. (DH)

Candlelight and Hot Dogs

Sometimes the fear of the unknown is stronger than the fear of what is known. For weeks my husband had been in a bad mood. Everything I did was "wrong." While I wanted to understand, Lee refused to confide in me. Nothing made any sense. *Did I do something I shouldn't have done?* I wondered. *Is God punishing me for something I did?*

One day Lee called me at lunchtime to apologize for blowing up at me the night before and then blew up at me again. He accused me of wanting a divorce. He was totally illogical, and I was afraid. Did *he* want a divorce?

Because I was afraid, I fumed. Then I prayed, *Lord, help me know what to do.* The Lord whispered to me, "Cook Lee a candlelight dinner."

Suddenly I felt like laughing. I giggled like a teenager getting ready for a date. I knew all we had in the freezer was hot dogs, but it didn't matter. I set a fancy table and sent the kids off to their rooms. As we ate the hot dogs by candlelight, we laughed and talked more than we had in weeks. Lee didn't tell me what bothered him, and I didn't ask. It just felt good to smile again.

As I read my Bible the next morning, I looked up verses on fear. The Scriptures show that Jesus often told his disciples and others not to be afraid. One passage that I return to the most is Mark's account of Jesus' being asleep in the boat as a storm came up. The disciples had no idea what was to happen to them. Even though they went to Jesus in fear, he helped them and calmed the storm. The day after our candlelight dinner, I prayed: *Lord, I give you my fear. Please give me your peace.* I'm sure God could have given me a lecture such as "What do you think I've been waiting to do?" but he didn't. He gave me peace.

A short time later, on our ninth wedding anniversary, my forty-one-year-old husband was diagnosed with Alzheimer's disease, which has as one of its symptoms illogical behavior. When I learned this and began to face the reality of dealing with the illness, I was able to thank the Lord that he had calmed my fears and had given me the courage to respond to Lee's anger and frustration with love and a candlelight dinner.

Let God calm your fears as well. If the unknowns of your caregiving cause you to be afraid, remember that God has promised to calm those fears.

"I sought the LORD, and he answered me; he delivered me from all my fears" (Ps. 34:4).

Thank you, heavenly Father, for letting me know that no matter what the circumstances are, I can trust you, and you will calm the storms. (MAM)

Leaning Hard

This was a totally new, an incredibly intimidating scenario—one which grabbed me completely out of my comfort zone.

In the Philippines, as in many other countries, hospitals require a family member or "helper" to stay with the patient. Lacking any nurses' aides, the hospital depends on this extra help for the patient for routine duties such as assisting with feeding, brushing teeth, monitoring fluid intake, or fetching and cleaning bedpans.

Even as a child, I had never wanted to be a nurse when I grew up. I didn't like any part of the duties of nursing. Besides, I had been totally turned off about the idea of a medical career by an experience when I was eight years old. My mom had taken me to our family's eye/ear/nose and throat specialist to find out the reason for my frequent sore throats and ear infections. Dr. Dudman asked me to follow him from his office to a room with special testing equipment. As we passed a more-than-half-opened door, I glanced at the man sitting on the examining table and was repulsed by what appeared to be only half of his upper face intact. After that view of exposed tissue, bone, and muscle, I vowed to avoid any such situation in the future.

The day after Bob's stroke, a nurse informed me that my husband needed a particular medicine. Because the hospital did not have it, I would need to go out into the city to find and purchase it. I was given no clues about where to locate this medication. A Filipino friend provided transportation so we could go to every medical-type place in the huge city of Manila, but we couldn't come up with the requested pills.

Close to tears and sure that my failure might prove life-threatening for

Bob, I reported to the nurse on the evening shift. She sort of shrugged her shoulders and replied: "Oh, Doctora Collado said it really isn't important."

And that was only one of many times when I felt my equilibrium being eaten away by feelings of frustration, confusion, and inadequacy. This was such a new and unfamiliar assignment!

How thankful I was—and am—that I can lean hard on an absolutely adequate heavenly Father. How mind-boggling yet reassuring to know that he understands my feelings and is able to care for all of them.

"The Lord himself goes before you and will be with you; he will never leave you nor forsake you. Do not be afraid; do not be discouraged" (Deut. 31:8).

What an awesome God you are! Tough, yet tender; majestic, yet merciful. Remind me often, Lord, of the character qualities that tell me who you are and who you want to be in my life. Remind me to let go of my own inadequate feelings so I *can* lean heavily on your perfection. (LDV)

The "Other" Help

For most caregivers, there is a moment when reality strikes. After days or weeks of whirling thoughts and fears, a silent moment comes. Maybe it is in the hospital bathroom or behind the wheel of your car or down a grocery aisle—wherever it is, in that unclamoring moment, the magnitude of your changed life hits you with billboard clarity.

Few of us can handle that moment without doing something—stopping, sucking air, grabbing for support, or thinking, *How can I ever do this?*

My moment came after my husband was recovering from his first cancer surgery. I'd been in and out of the hospital. I'd gone home and told the kids, "Daddy's okay but . . ." I'd spent a night alone in our queen-size bed. I'd eaten a meal with an empty chair across from me. And I'd answered a few "How is he?" phone calls. But always my mind raced with replays of the past days or fears for the future.

That race miraculously stopped one day when I entered the hospital. Without asking for directions or glancing at the arrow signs, I'd gone up in the elevator, maneuvered through the maze of halls, and pushed open the stainless steel doors of the surgery ward. As I registered the now familiar smell of antiseptic over illness, it hit. My hands froze on the steel and I stopped.

This was my life.

Involuntarily my mind cried out, *Oh Lord, how will I ever make it?*

It was as if God lifted my head and opened my eyes. I saw a patient walking with a portable IV pole. I saw a nurse sitting at the center station. I saw a lab technician with his red tray of vials. I saw a cleaning lady come out of a room. Then God whispered, "You'll only get through this by thinking of them and not just you."

I let the doors swing closed behind me and started walking toward my husband's room. Without one doubt, I knew God was right. My mind would always automatically focus on me and mine in the crisis of change. Unless I deliberately looked out to see others once in a while, my inner focus on our tragedy would defeat me.

"Therefore comfort each other and edify one another, just as you also are doing" (1 Thess. 5:11, NKJV).

No wonder you have so many "one anothers" in Scripture, Lord. It's not just for your sake and their sake. It is for my sake too. (DH)

The Presence of God

Sometimes learning the shocking truth can actually be a relief. After months of wondering and worrying, knowing what is wrong can diminish confusion.

I was in shock when I learned what was wrong with my husband. However, I was also relieved. After three months of tests, I finally had an answer to Lee's strange and often illogical behavior. The doctor told me my forty-one-year-old husband probably had Alzheimer's disease. (The only completely accurate diagnosis is based on an autopsy.)

Immediately I went to the library to search for information on this disease. I read about all the things that would take place over the next few years. I cried for the husband I was losing and for myself. There was no place for me to run away and hide.

That weekend between reading the chapters, I paced the floor and cried out to God for understanding. Then I remembered a time when our dog Windy was about to have her puppies. When we arrived home after an all-day outing, she barked to come into the house. Then she whined and scratched to go out. This went on for several minutes until I finally got her message.

She needed to be outside to have her pups, but she wanted me to be there with her. It didn't bother Windy that it was raining and cold outside. She lay against the house under the eaves. I grabbed a heavy blanket and wrapped up in it and sat on the ground next to her. I petted her and talked to her, even sang to her. She relaxed and had her puppies.

Suddenly, it dawned on me: I was acting like Windy, needing to be with someone in a time of crisis. Yet God was already there waiting to talk to me, rub my back, and even sing to me. I just had to find a spot to collapse and listen. As I did, God promised me that he would be with me through every step of this disease—and he has been.

If you are dealing with something new, learn all you can about it. It does help to know what to expect. Even more important, however, is to remember that God will go through this time with you. As the poem about the footprints in the sand reminds us, God carries us when we are too weak to carry ourselves.

"The Lord will give strength to his people; the Lord will bless his people with peace" (Ps. 29:11, NASB).

Thank you, Lord, for your daily love and support. (MAM)

Good Days

Though caregiving brings physical exhaustion and emotional turmoil, not every moment is filled with difficulties. There are many days when the routine goes well, good friends visit, laughs are shared, and God feels so close you can almost touch him.

During these times, the situation doesn't seem so bad. Everyone is adjusting. It almost feels like things are returning to "normal." But then the person you're caring for looks a bit uncomfortable and shifts in his or her seat. Or the phone rings and you hear the voice of your doctor or the woman who comes in on Wednesdays. Inside you freeze, trying to prepare yourself. What new circumstance is now trying to knock you off your emotional feet?

Even if the uncomfortable shift or phone call proves to be nothing, your mind will have already asked, *What is it this time? What's coming next?* I don't know how often my "little fear freezes" robbed me of a day's goodness.

Most of the time I didn't realize how they caused me to suppress my contentment as I threw up my guard against the next dark moment. Or how they caused me to expect the good to end. I knew bad news or another difficulty was just around the corner.

A good example of such fear robbery happened on an early fall day. Art felt well enough for us to walk along the lake by our country home, so we set out to enjoy the season. The leaves were turning into light and fire while the afternoon sun triggered warm blackberry smells. We enjoyed the lapping water and tail-ended ducks. But then I saw Art reach up and rub his lower back.

The sights, the smells, the sounds disappeared in a moment. In their place were thoughts of spreading cancer, another doctor visit, and how long we had left together. The rest of our walk I registered very little around us.

God never actually "lectured" me about my negative mindset. Perhaps he understood that it just went along with caring for someone who was sick. But from time to time, he'd bring a Scripture passage to mind that I'd memorized as a child.

> *"Which of you by worrying can add one cubit to his stature? . . . Therefore do not worry about tomorrow, for tomorrow will worry about its own things. Sufficient for the day is its own trouble" (Matt. 6:27,34, NKJV).*

Lord, you are a good God. Your Word declares it. Help me live in the presence of goodness when it comes, not lose it in tomorrow's worries. (DH)

Walking through Fear

So many things rouse fear when the one you love needs your care. Each of us faces our own circumstances and our own unique fears. Yet, over and over again, we see that Jesus said, "Fear not!" Does this sound like a suggestion . . . or a command?

If it's a command, how can we obey?

One very special lady gave me a powerful answer to this question. Pat suffered from panic attacks—the most severe, uncontrollable of fears—which made her a prisoner in her own home. Finally, even her home terrified her. She was afraid to step into her own shower. This was no small fear; she says she was as panic-stricken as if she were confronted by a raging bear that was about to grab her.

Pat prayed. She was on medication and under a doctor's care. But nothing eased her panic. At the same time, despite the severity of her attacks, she had managed to hide them from her family by making some believable excuses for not going out. She was afraid they would think she was crazy if she told them the truth.

Then one day her husband came home excited because his parents wanted them to accompany them to the World's Fair. This meant hours of travel in an RV, camping overnight, and being in crowds of people. Pat gasped, "Oh, I just don't feel like going. You can go without me." Disappointment dimmed his smile, but he accepted her decision with his usual kindness.

After he left the room, Pat thought of the fun they used to have together and of how long it had been since she had gone anywhere with her husband. Her behavior wasn't fair to him. Somehow she must try to go this time. She prayed, "Lord, I want to go. Please help me." Then, acting on faith, she went to tell her husband she would go.

Through prayer and trust, she survived the long drive and sleeping in a strange place, but with her first glimpse of the hundreds of people milling about in the walkways of the fairgrounds, she froze. Panic swept over her. Her grip on her husband's hand tightened, but she only told him, "I just need to stop and rest a minute."

Silently and desperately she prayed, *Help me, Lord. Hold my hand just like my husband is holding my hand. If you hold my hand I can go on.* In her mind she imagined Jesus standing right beside her, holding her hand. *Okay, Lord, I'm going to take one step. Hold my hand.* One step at a time, imagining Jesus holding her hand, Pat walked out of her panic.

They had a wonderful time at the fair, and when Pat got home she methodically visited each place that had provoked panic attacks, such as the grocery store, the post office, the bank. As she left the house, she would say, "Here we go again, Lord. Hold my hand." Then she imagined him doing just that. By this vivid use of her faith, in a few days she conquered her illness and began to live fearlessly.

She was not playing games or relying on positive thinking. She was practicing a truth from the Bible—Jesus said he would be with us to the ends of the earth. Why should we think he won't come to be beside us in a sick room, a doctor's waiting room, a hospital room, or at the dawn of another day of uncertainty? He is here right beside us as he promised.

In Pat's desperation, she found a special way to trust in the Lord. Now, when I am afraid, I invariably remember Pat and say her words. "Hold my hand, Lord. Okay, here we go."

"Surely I am with you always, to the very end of the age" (Matt. 28:20).

"Christ be with me, Christ before me, Christ behind me, Christ in me, Christ beneath me, Christ above me, Christ on my right, Christ on my left, Christ where I lie, Christ where I sit, Christ where I arise. . . . Salvation is of Christ. May your salvation, Lord, be ever with us." *A prayer of St. Patrick* (EL)

Dealing with the Fear

After Lee went on disability because of Alzheimer's, I faced fears about making it alone, about whether I would have people there to support me, about money matters, about finding my own time with friends, and about being excluded by other couples from their plans.

Our friends the Garlands had moved to Oregon before us. They had been wonderful in helping us get settled, but the worse Lee became, the less I heard from them. I learned once from some mutual friends who had been visiting that the Garlands had driven them by our house to show them where we lived, but they had not stopped. I felt so utterly hurt. I tried calling them a couple of times to make plans to get together, but they were always too busy. I never heard from them again. My fears of rejection because of this disease seemed to be coming true. I had to accept the fact that some people could not deal with Lee's deterioration. It hurt, but I asked God to help me understand, and he has.

As we read the Bible, we learn that even if all our friends leave us, God will not abandon us. We can give him all our fears. Holding on to Christ, we can live one day at a time. Yesterday is gone. Nothing in the past can be changed. Tomorrow has not yet come. But today God holds us up and gives us strength.

"Fear thou not; for I am with thee: be not dismayed; for I am thy God: I will strengthen thee; yea, I will help thee" (Isa. 41:10, KJV).

Thank you, Father, for today's strength. (MAM)

Take Courage

What can give us courage in the face of those sit-down-and-hold-on-to-yourself fears that haunt us as caregivers? We must get to know God better, by prayer, by study, by any and every means, but sometimes we receive courage first from other people like ourselves.

Phillips Brooks, a New England preacher of the last century who wrote the beloved Christmas carol "O Little Town of Bethlehem," suggests we can take courage from all the Christians who have gone before us. We are so fortunate to have the writings of many who have left strong testimonies of their own courage in Christ. Brooks says that we are only tracing over in our own blood what earlier people wrote in theirs. In Volume 1 of his sermons, he says, "Do not misread history, that it shall seem to you when you try to do the right, as if you were the first person that ever tried it. Put yourself with your weak little struggle into the company of all the strugglers in all time."

This early concept of what we now might call a "support group" can give us a better perspective. Reading about and remembering God-loving people who have struggled does build up our courage.

Knowing someone here and now helps as well. In my family, I watched my mother care for her bedfast mother in our home the last seven years of Grandma's life. Then I watched her care for my father for more than four years when he could no longer walk. At that time Mom was bent over with Parkinson's disease. The doctor urged her to place Dad in a nursing home, but she determined to make his last days as pleasant as possible by keeping him at home. Watching her often so tired, I grieved over the burden she had taken upon herself. I learned, however, that what I saw as a burden was something else to her.

Several years after Dad died, I was with Mom on the anniversary of his death. I didn't mention it, not knowing if she wanted to talk about it. She finally said, "It's been three years since your papa died."

"Yes, I know. I remembered the day, but it doesn't seem that long ago!"

"It does to me." She didn't elaborate, but I remembered the last kiss she had placed on his lips when we went to view him in the funeral home.

I wished I could take back my thoughtless remark. They'd had sixty-four loving years together, and her love for him made his absence seem longer than three years. I could see she would gladly return to that caregiving if she could. Her love for him had given her the courage to become his caregiver and to face all the uncertainties involved. Mom showed me that long-term courage comes from love. And her faith in God showed me the source of her love that never failed.

Whether or not we know the details, we can be sure that somewhere in our family history is a long record of caregiving, for this is the way families have functioned through the ages. If we know their stories, we can take courage from their love and commitment. If we don't know our family histories, we can take courage from many stories from others.

Take heart! God still cares and will supply what we need when we need it.

"He will fulfill the desires of those who reverently and worshipfully fear him; he also will hear their cry and will save them" (Ps. 145:19, AMP).

Heavenly Father, thank you for the love that has passed from generation to generation through our family traditions of caring for our own. Thank you for the courage to grasp this opportunity to be your stand-in—to be your love with skin on—for our loved ones. (EL)

Strength in His Roots

At times, life seems overwhelming. It seems if there isn't one crisis, there's another just waiting to claim our time. One of those times for me was the day the doctor completed all her tests on Lee. I was so overwhelmed with all that had happened. I paced the house reliving Dr. Reed's words. She had told me my husband needed to go on disability retirement due to Alzheimer's disease. I'd gotten a book at the library and read all the things that could happen to Lee. The tears just wouldn't stop.

Walking by my kitchen window, I stopped pacing and found myself staring at a linden tree I'd planted some years before. I'd hoped it would eventually give shade to that window. I began remembering—the times when our children and their friends had accidentally broken off many of the thin branches; another time when someone had come into our yard and stomped in the middle of the tree, breaking all the branches; and another time when our dog had knocked off the whole top of the young tree with her chain, leaving only the trunk. Each time something had happened, I had been sure that that was the end of the tree. But always the following spring it would again burst forth with new leaves and new branches.

Now my life felt like that linden—broken and trampled. As I continued to stare at the tree, God reminded me of Psalm 27:1 (below). I did not need to be afraid of this disease or of the future without Lee. As time went on, everywhere I searched in the Bible, God showed me how he brings help and comfort in every kind of trouble. I became more and more sure that whatever the future held, I could look to God's promise of hope and joy without fear, despair, or desperation. God strengthened my roots.

He also surprised me with areas of strength and ability in myself. Seven years after that tearful day at my kitchen window, Lee went into the nursing home and I returned to college. I learned new skills and began to write. God continued to show me daily that he was and is going to make my roots stronger in him.

When I later returned to my old house for a visit, I saw that the battered tree had grown tall and strong. On the days when you feel weak, try to remember that through Christ your roots are also strong. God loves all of us. He isn't going to give just some of us the strong roots we need to go through difficult situations. He will do it for all of us.

"The Lord is my light and my salvation; whom shall I fear? The Lord is the strength of my life; of whom shall I be afraid?" (Ps. 27:1, NKJV).

Thank you, God, for the strength you give me. Thank you for stilling the fears of my heart. (MAM)

Fear's Hidden Blessing

Fear makes us want to flee, but when we stand up to fear and do what we are called to do, we discover a hidden joy.

In Matthew 5 Jesus talked to people about real happiness. I can imagine his excitement as he spoke those words—probably something like our delight when we plan a surprise for someone we love. Perhaps he could hardly wait for his listeners to unwrap the gift of joy he was offering.

Yet to many in the audience, his words must have sounded ludicrous. Today as well, the paths to joy that he described still run counter to popular opinion. Experts tell us that anyone who is poor in spirit probably has a poor self-image, a lack of confidence, and low self-esteem. Our culture prefers to believe: "Blessed are we when we have no deep needs, no unfulfilled desires, and no painful questions, and no one else depending on us."

Caregivers are called upon to break the world's rules for happiness. I think of long-term caregiving as a type of warfare. As the apostle Paul says, the battles we fight are against "principalities and unseen powers." I was inspired in my approach to this warfare by a letter of a young soldier in WW II who made a happy discovery during his battles.

Two months before he died in combat, John J. Hogan, an infantryman, wrote to his father:

> I was thinking tonight about the high spots of my life in the army. And synonymous with every such period is the name of a beachhead. . . . Of all the cherished experiences of my life, those have been the best which God blessed with the proximity of danger and possibility of death. . . . It is this paradox that makes Christianity a virile, exultant, unconquerable, eternal

life. It is God's own gift to us, the fruit of His Redemption and the fruit of His Resurrection. We grasp it rarely and with trembling hands, but when we do, we know with the almost blasphemous audacity of those who are reborn that we have touched the meaning of eternal life.

Hogan had an advantage over us—he knew he was in deadly combat. Our spiritual war can sometimes seem to be a series of minor, insignificant decisions. We can't always recognize or name our beachheads—the enemy territory we are in—but caregiving demands all we have to give.

In our case, however, the Lord is our defender. Even though we are exhausted, with Christ we can stand against doubt and fear, impatience and resentment, envy, or any other destructive attitude. In the grip of painful, unanswered questions, Christ sustains our mustard seed of faith. To know his strength—to live in his goodness in the midst of our battles is to be in the kingdom of heaven while still on earth.

On our silent beachheads, when the suffering of our loved ones threatens our faith, we too can find our highest experiences with God, and with trembling hands we can touch the mystery of the meaning of eternal life. This is the blessing—the beatitude—that comes from caregiving.

"You're blessed when you care. At the moment of being 'care-full,' you find yourselves cared for" (Matt. 5:7, THE MESSAGE).

Our Father, it's so easy to feel abandoned and frightened when things seem to go wrong. And yet I know you will never leave me alone. Patiently remind me of your presence and meet me at the sharp point of my need. I praise you for the blessing of victory over fear. (EL)

A Prayer Picture

Prayers come in all sizes, forms, and intensities when you are a caregiver. There are long prayers in which you pour out your heart to God. There are single-word prayers in which you only say, "Help!" In some prayers, your words seem to echo empty back into your ears. In others you can only ramble with disconnected thoughts. You also find yourself praying angry prayers, tearful ones, and praise-filled ones.

No matter what form they take, prayers are an essential part of taking care of another person. Even if you try to stop saying them, they unconsciously slip into your mind. You find yourself asking, demanding, pleading with God.

I prayed all types of non-prayers and prayers when my husband had cancer. Some made me feel better, but many did not. Yet I couldn't stop talking to the one who controlled my life, Art's life, and the lives of our children.

Talking to God so much made me wonder about what I really was doing when I prayed. I asked myself questions about prayer. I noticed sermons that spoke of it. And I even discussed it with others. Yet, nothing really satisfied me until I read about prayer in the book of Hebrews. The fourth chapter talks about a high priest who sympathizes with our weaknesses and provides the privilege of confidently coming to the throne of grace when we feel needy.

This passage brought a new picture of prayer into my mind. When I talked to God, I started visualizing myself walking into the very throne room of heaven. I'd see myself before God's throne. Sometimes I just talked with him. Sometimes I fell on my knees before him. Sometimes I crawled into his lap and cried on his shoulder. More than once I even imagined myself carrying Art into his presence and putting the man I loved into his arms.

These prayers came to mean so much to me—they made talking to God real. They brought comfort even when I felt my deepest hurts and cried my hardest tears.

> *"For we do not have a High Priest who cannot sympathize with our weaknesses, but was in all points tempted as we are, yet without sin. Let us therefore come boldly to the throne of grace, that we may obtain mercy and find grace to help in time of need"* (Heb. 4:15-16, NKJV).

I can't see you, touch you, or smell you, Lord. So sometimes talking to you doesn't seem real. Please, remind me what your Word says. Remind me that every prayer takes me into your very presence. (DH)

Comfort in Grief

One of my treasures is a piece of petrified wood. On the outside it looks ugly—
it's a rough, dull, brown rock. Someone, suspecting beauty within, cut into its
heart, smoothed a flat surface, and polished it. Rich russets, golds, and blue
grays swirl into the shape of a mysterious landscape. We keep this petrified
wood on a counter where we can gaze at it often and run our fingers over the
flawless polished surface.

I have found that grief is like that petrified wood—rough, ugly, and unde-
sirable on the outside, yet beautiful within. Grief only comes to people who
love, and yet to love is to be favored with joy beyond mere happiness. If that is
true for the love of weak human beings, imagine the case if we could possibly
love as God loves us; we would be filled with a happiness so big it could
scarcely be contained by our human hearts.

Modern physicians have said Jesus' heart literally ruptured while he hung
on the cross. I wonder—did his heart break only from the grief of bearing our
sins? Or did it also break from love so big that his human body could not con-
tain it?

Shall I grieve because of the suffering Jesus endured for me, or shall I rejoice because he loves me so much? In considering this, I have to acknowledge
the whole of grief: the outer crust of pain and the hidden inside part, which is
the joy of love.

John Bunyan, author of *Pilgrim's Progress,* said, "Of all tears, they are
best that are made by the blood of Christ; and of all joy, that is sweetest, that is
mixed with mourning over Christ. Oh! it is a goodly thing to be on our knees
with Christ in our arms, before God."

Look for the beauty of loving contained within sorrow. Thank God for the love he gives, which can redeem every agonizing situation.

"Those who are sad now are happy. God will comfort them" (Matt. 5:4, NCV).

Heavenly Father, your Son promised comfort for me when I mourn. Remembering him I ask you to comfort me now. Please fill me with your love and grant me a peaceful, trusting heart. (EL)

The Positive Side of Questions

For most people queries such as "How are you doing?" are no big deal. But for the caregiver, questions about health, with their resulting advice or "My uncle had that too" stories, can get old. It isn't that you don't love the people for asking and sharing; it's just that it's hard to know what or how to answer all the time.

Do you really tell friends and family that the tests show no improvement and you're discouraged or angry? And if you do, doesn't repeating it a dozen times make the situation just that much harder to deal with? It's a no-win situation. You need the love and concern of others, but you don't want to keep saying the same things over and over. You wish you could find a perfect, single answer that would take care of all the questions.

There were many times in my caregiving experience when I felt like this. Whenever possible I gave the answering job to others, letting them get the phone or the front door. But too often, perhaps going to church or to my children's school, I couldn't escape the inevitable questions: "How are you doing?" "Are the kids OK?" "What do the latest tests show?"

I wanted a pat answer so badly, I even prayed and asked God for one. But I received no magic phrase that would release me from those unavoidable queries. It was as if God said, "There is no easy shortcut. Person by person, you must trust me to deal with each question."

The questions never did get easy, but God used them. They taught me honesty when I had to say, "I'm sorry, but I just can't bear to go through it again. Could you ask Cheryl; she knows the latest." They revealed which friends didn't know what to say. They helped me process my anger, my pain, my doubts. They motivated me to ask for help from others. They made me say, "I'm sorry for how I spoke to you." And they made me rely on God.

Caregiving with all its questions is a trial of faith, and we can take great comfort in the promise that Jesus made to his disciples. God will give us words when we need them.

> *"Now when they bring you to the synagogues and magistrates and authorities, do not worry about how or what you should answer, or what you should say. For the Holy Spirit will teach you in that very hour what you ought to say"* (Luke 12:11-12, NKJV).

Lord, answering questions is so hard right now. But somehow, in some way, show me when to speak and what to say today. (DH)

Good News

One thing I'm sure you've learned about caring for someone: Money doesn't always spread as far as we think it should.

The first Christmas after Lee went on disability retirement, there just wasn't any money available to buy presents for our six children or to prepare fancy holiday dinners. We weren't going to have a tree, and I didn't feel like digging out any decorations. Worse than that, I was sure no one cared about my family or what we were going through.

Then, three weeks before Christmas, a friend from church asked Lee and me to visit his Sunday school class. When we arrived, the class presented us with a small evergreen tree covered with tiny decorations, small envelopes, and a handmade needlepoint mailbox. They told us to take these things home and open the envelopes with our children.

Our oldest child was away at college, but the other five children, Lee, and I sat around the kitchen table and opened envelope after envelope. The ones, fives, tens, and twenties added up to over two hundred dollars. They had told us to open the mailbox last. Inside we found a check from the class for one hundred dollars and instructions that this money was to be spent only on Christmas presents.

Overwhelmed by this love shown to us, I cried, but for the first time in several months I was weeping tears of joy. God had kept his promise. He hadn't forsaken us!

God's good news didn't end there, however. A few days before Christmas, we received a basket from my husband's former employer, which included all the fixings for our holiday dinner, plus presents for the children.

Then, each day until the twenty-fifth, we continued to receive baskets of groceries from various families.

For the first time in several months, our cupboards overflowed. All this food lasted until April when escrow closed on our house and we moved from Southern California to Oregon. It was my first lesson in learning God would take care of us, and he has continued to do so.

Do you remember the first time God supplied your needs? Let God's faithfulness in supplying your needs in the past comfort you now. Hold onto that important event, and thank God for it. If you have an object you can use as a visible reminder of that time, great. But most of all, remember God does love you, and he will supply your needs.

"In the day when I cried out, you answered me, and made me bold with strength in my soul" (Ps. 138:3, NKJV).

Heavenly Father, no matter what other Christmases may hold for me, the little country mailbox decoration on our tree will always remind me that you do love and care for me through people who also care. (MAM)

Need a Listening Ear?

Do you yearn for a listening ear, for genuine attention, for meaningful communication with the one you care for?

My husband and I drew together in significant new ways when his post-stroke pain and frustration became *my* daily companions. Some days, some weeks, though, the Stroke-Intruder seems to sweep away any meaningful moments. Partly because of Bob's lack of hearing and focus, and mainly because of that wasted dark area of his brain, communication barely exists sometimes. My need for communication remains despite the circumstances, and this has driven me to seek, and find, God's listening ear.

Tim Hansel said in his book *You Gotta Keep Dancing,*

> One of the greatest tragedies of our modern civilization is that you and I can live a trivial life and get away with it. One of the great advantages of pain and suffering is that it forces us to break through our superficial crusts to discover life on a deeper and more meaningful level.

My husband's disabling stroke provoked me to turn to God, rather than to superficial answers, in crisis times. Discover, as I have, the joyful reality of God's full attention and cherishing. How? By asking and expecting and believing . . . and listening! I've gotten in the habit now of mentally climbing up in the Lord's lap and pouring out my heart to him, knowing that he listens lovingly and attentively.

How thankful I am that God always has time for us. In fact, he delights in you and me.

"The Lord your God is with you, he is mighty to save. He will take great delight in you, he will quiet you with his love, he will rejoice over you with singing" (Zeph. 3:17).

Thank you for loving us so deeply and for listening so attentively, heavenly Father. I ask that I might make full use of the precious privileges that come with being a member of your forever-family. Amen. (LDV)

Forgetting, But Not Forgotten

Three years after my dad died, my mother needed live-in care. Parkinson's disease had paralyzed her legs. I and my sisters—Dorothy, Edith, and Alice—took turns staying with her for two days at a stretch. After several more years, Mom's memory faded. Most of the time she didn't know she was in her own home. She even forgot who I was. I feared she also had forgotten God.

I grieved because now, when she most needed her faith, it might not be sustaining her at all. As long as she had been able, she'd sat at the dining room east window and read her devotional books and prayed most of each morning. With her disease so advanced she could no longer do this.

As I watched her slip away from us and from the strength of her faith, I yelled at God a lot. "She deserves better than this! Look at all the good she's done for others!"

One afternoon as Mom and I sat together in the living room, she closed her eyes and seemed to doze off, as she often did. Then she began to moan. My mother had never complained in her life. She had endured all pain, fear, and worry silently. Alarmed, I rushed to her. When I touched her shoulder, she jumped and opened startled eyes. "Are you in pain?" I asked.

She stared at me, looking puzzled. Parkinson's disease had made speech very difficult for her. She struggled to find her voice and then to make her tongue and lips form words. "No. I don't hurt anywhere."

I asked her more questions, trying to discover what she needed, but she insisted she didn't need anything. So I sat down again. Mom closed her eyes and soon began to moan once more. When I went to her, she acted startled and almost looked irritated at being bothered. After questioning her several times, I could only sit and let her moan until she fell asleep. That evening when my sister Edith arrived to stay, I told her about the moaning, hoping she would be able to make Mom comfortable.

Several days later when I returned, Edith said, "Oh, by the way, I found out why Mom was moaning. She finally told me she was praying. She said it twice."

I could have wept for joy. Mom had forgotten who I was, but she remembered God! And she remembered how to pray even though she couldn't speak the words. I knew God was listening with his most tender love, for "the Spirit helps us in our weakness. We do not know what we ought to pray for, but the Spirit himself intercedes for us with groans that words cannot express" (Rom. 8:26).

To the last week of her life, Mom's memory would flash back to us briefly, and although she didn't recognize me, her youngest, she knew my older sisters. Since she had known God longer than she had known me, I feel certain her faith in God comforted her to the end.

The greater blessing in our life stories is that even if our loved ones can't remember God, he will never forget them. Nor will he disregard our prayers or forget us in our struggles to assist those we love. We can rest our aching hearts in this truth.

"Are not five sparrows sold for two copper coins? And not one of them is forgotten before God. But the very hairs of your head are all numbered. Do not fear therefore; you are of more value than many sparrows" (Luke 12:6-7, NKJV).

Lord, what a comfort it is to know that you never, never forget us. What a comfort that you yourself—through your Spirit—pray for us even when we can't think what to pray. What a win-win opportunity! You created us to be failure-free at prayer! Please make this fact real to us and to our loved ones. Amen. (EL)

Shared Sorrow

A Swedish proverb says "Shared joy is double joy and shared sorrow is half a sorrow."

Most of my life I've kept the hard times to myself. I didn't want anyone to know of my difficulties. The first time someone suggested a support group after Lee had gone on disability, I felt very uncomfortable. I began going to the group, but sat alone, too ashamed to share what was on my heart.

Then one day after the meeting, I went up to someone and asked her how she was doing. After a few sentences from her, I began to open up. Suddenly we were in each other's arms crying. She knew how I felt, and I knew how she felt. I went home feeling better than I had in weeks. I had shared with someone who understood.

Since then, I've realized my sharing is important to others, as well as to me. I've learned to be available so others can speak as well as listen to me.

God understands our need to be understood. When Mary and Martha met Jesus after Lazarus died, he shared their sorrow and pain, and I know he shares our pain personally, as well as through the caring human beings around us.

"Two are better than one, because they have a good reward for their toil. For if they fall, one will lift up the other" (Eccles. 4:9-10, NRSV).

God, thank you for understanding my pain. Thank you for listening when I talk. (MAM)

Enjoy the Blessing

Have you ever felt as if you were cheated out of some special activity because of your caregiving?

Before Lee went into a nursing home, it became more and more difficult for us to do things as a family. I remember one Fourth of July—the kids wanted to go see the fireworks display, but because Lee had been quite agitated all day, I didn't think it would be a good idea to take him out. I was exhausted after a trying day and wanted to enjoy the celebration also, but I didn't want to have to choose who could go and who had to stay home with Lee, so we all stayed home. My kids were angry and I was depressed.

We had a large picture window in our living room that faced the Cascade mountain range. About the time the fireworks were to go on display at the fairgrounds, the sky to the east over the mountains lit up with God's own fireworks. The most beautiful lightning I'd ever seen lasted for about thirty minutes, and we had our own quiet family celebration.

I truly believe God cares about the little things such as fireworks displays in our lives. As I thought about our experience later, I was reminded of Elijah. When he suffered from depression, God sent food and water to him where he was. While my reason for staying home was different than Elijah's, the same God supplies my needs.

Charles Haddon Spurgeon once said, "Somewhere or other in the worst flood of trouble there is always a dry spot for contentment to get its foot on, and if there were not, it would learn to swim."

Look for this dry spot and then grab on to the little joys in life. Sometimes even the biggest events are eclipsed by memories of such little things.

"Come and see the works of the Lord" (Ps. 46:8).

Thank you, Father, for caring enough about me to give me my own fireworks show in your lightning and for always providing a dry spot in the midst of the flood. (MAM)

Holy Comparison

Every caregiver has heard it or perhaps even told it to themselves. Yet there are few things that grate on our mental chalkboard more than the words, "Her son can't even move. You [or I] should be thankful that yours is able to do things."

There is no comfort in comparing hardships. The fears, the exhaustion, the emotional strain, the changed relationships—these take place in every caregiving situation and cannot be diminished by saying one circumstance is worse than another. All such comparison does is make you feel defensive toward the person speaking or guilty about yourself because you aren't "handling" things better.

There is one exception. Recently I received a note from a friend with a disabled son who was undergoing some corrective surgery at a famous children's hospital. He wrote, "We have learned one thing through all of this—there are many others who are suffering with health problems that plague their family members. We've seen babies with heart maladies, teens with cancer, head trauma, and generally patients who are worse off than our son. We pray for the others!"

This note reminded me that when the Holy Spirit points out other situations, the chalk draws smoothly in our minds as he shows us a clear picture. Instead of raising defensive walls or feeling guilty, we really see the other people. We are moved to care and to pray, in spite of our own hardship.

Each of us as caregivers will face comparison in one form or another. When it comes, we'll try to deal with it. But sometimes we won't be able to, and we'll need a divine hand to change the impossible.

"For mortals it is impossible, but for God all things are possible" (Matt. 19:26, NRSV).

Lord, help me to let go of comparisons, my own and other people's. Only your Spirit has the perfect voice to make me hear with my heart. (DH)

Preserved from Depression

The exhaustion I experienced all week seemed way out of proportion to the physical demands of caregiving. Working in the garden usually helped to ease my tensions and tiredness, but after Bob's stroke even this favorite activity left me feeling stale and weary. I remembered my doctor's recent question: "Do you think you are depressed?" Of course I gave a negative answer. I was supposed to be the strong one now, wasn't I?

Since the beginning of my married life I had taken pleasure in growing and preserving delicious berries and vegetables. Those old patterns cause me still to pickle and jam and freeze and can a lot more than the two of us can eat for the next decade or so! I seem to feel a compulsion to do *something* with whatever is in season.

Late last summer I was making a batch of blackberry jam (berries courtesy of my grandson, who put more of the fragrant globs into his mouth than he did into the pail!) when I discovered a shortage of jam jars. Only two empty ones remained after my frenzied summer of preserving. So I hastily gathered together any available container—a glass cream pitcher, assorted cups and mugs, water glasses. Then I poured in the bubbling purple liquid and watched how beautifully the jam assumed the shape of each.

That afternoon I told my husband about my surrogate jam jars, so we could share a smile together. I also passed along the thought that God had whispered to me earlier: Just as the jam flowed to fill each container's curves, God's grace assumes the shape of our most difficult circumstances—even as it was filling me up already. Realizing this, I felt less tired and depleted. The depression lifted.

As I see the flowering trees bursting into frothy bloom each spring, I'm reminded of God's grace in a similar way. Those lovely clouds of blossoms turn the ugliest house or yard into a "beauty mark." It happens suddenly, without evidence of special attention, and is totally undeserved—like God's grace!

The Lord's grace shapes itself perfectly to the varied forms of our daily experiences. Whether we are dealing with depression or terminal illness or dementia or loneliness, God's loving grace fits them all.

"My grace is sufficient for you, for my power is made perfect in weakness" (2 Cor. 12:9).

Thanks for knowing how much it helps us, Lord, to have tangible illustrations to make clear your deep truths. Like grace! Now I'm reminded of the delights and the importance of your grace every time I spoon strawberry jam on Bob's English muffin or spread apricot preserves on my toast. (LDV)

Finding Peace

Because of the busy and demanding lives we live as caregivers, we long for serenity and peace to surround our days and hours. I've discovered, though, that peace doesn't mean a lack of tension or concern; it simply means we can honestly say, "It's okay." Peace comes not from the absence of conflict in our lives, but from the ability to cope with conflict.

The Lord says, "Do not be anxious about anything, but in everything, by prayer and petition, with thanksgiving, present your requests to God. And the peace of God, which transcends all understanding, will guard your hearts and your minds in Christ Jesus" (Phil. 4:6-7).

You and I want *external* answers to prayer, but verse 7 of Philippians chapter 4 promises *internal* answers. We are unable to receive the promise of verse 7 until we follow the precepts of verse 6.

Prayer warrior Andrew Murray wrote:

Time spent in prayer will yield more than that given to work. Prayer alone gives work its worth and its success. Prayer opens the way for God himself to do his work in us and through us. Let our chief work as God's messengers be intercession; in it we secure the presence and power of God to go with us.

The fourteenth chapter of the Gospel of John is full of comfort and promises for us, and toward the end Jesus clarifies the kind of peace he is talking about: "Peace I leave with you; my peace I give you. I do not give to you as the world gives. Do not let your hearts be troubled and do not be afraid" (vv. 14:27).

I'll settle for that kind of peace any day!

"You will keep in perfect peace him whose mind is steadfast, because he trusts in you. Trust in the LORD forever, for the LORD, the LORD, is the Rock eternal" (Isa. 26:3-4).

As I look out the window and see the majestic oak straining in the October wind, Lord, I know that on the windward side the tree will be sending down a deeper root, to add strength for future winds. Thank you that in a similar way, through prayer and unconditional trust in you, I can ready myself for future trials and conflicts. (LDV)

One Quick Prayer

During the years I was a single parent before I married Lee, I often faced problems that I was sure I wouldn't have if I had a husband to take care of me. One such time came when I'd just learned to drive at age thirty. My nine-year-old son was playing on the floor of the living room with his toys spread all around him when I heard a knock at our back door. A neighbor told me that there was water all over the ground under my car. I'd had my first car, a used one, for only a month. I knew nothing about cars except how to drive one.

My son and I had recently moved. The only people we knew were my brother and his family who were out of town for a few days, and Rex, a young man who'd worked with me in the junior high department of our church the year before. I had to get to work the next day. What was I to do?

I thought of calling a gas station mechanic, but I'd heard too many stories about how they loved to "rip off" women who know nothing about cars. My next thought was to phone Rex, but his number wasn't listed in the phone book. There was only one thing I could do—pray! It was only one short quick prayer, *Lord, please send Rex.*

I sensed assurance from God that Rex would come. Then I did something I'd never done before; I acted on my prayer. I turned to Bruce and told him to clean up because Rex was coming over. When he asked me how I knew, I simply told him, "Because I prayed and asked God to send him."

Wide-eyed, Bruce began to pick up his toys.

Forty-five minutes later when the doorbell rang I knew it could only be one person. I could have hugged Rex when I opened the door, but I didn't think he would understand. Instead, I simply invited him to come in. He was looking for my brother, but I didn't care what his reason was; I knew God had sent him. We talked for a few minutes, and then I told him about the water under my car.

Rex checked and found a broken water hose. Ten minutes before the auto parts store closed, Rex, the last customer of the day, got the hose, and then he replaced the broken one.

My faith in prayer became a lot stronger that night. God also helped a nine-year-old boy discover that his heavenly Father cares about the little things and he answers prayer. The next time a problem came up, Bruce was the one to suggest, "Mom, we need to pray about this."

Since then I've learned to pray about every situation, and I'm so glad God is there to listen and answer.

"And God is able to make all grace abound to you" (2 Cor. 9:8).

Father, thank you that you do take care of us—single parents, caregivers, and nine-year-old boys. (MAM)

An Eternal Run

One of the hardest aspects of caregiving is watching someone we love deal with the frustration and pain of broken health. Whether we watch a child with birth defects struggling to read or a frail parent struggling to walk, their plight becomes ours. We want it to be easier for them. We want to do something, anything, to ease their striving.

I often felt that way as I watched my husband go from running twenty easy miles a week, to laboring through ten tough ones, to walking in place while hanging on to an IV pole. At times I thought of his pre-cancer body. Long and lithe, it ate up mile after mile with a fluid motion that made running seem as easy as a bird's flight. But eventually my mind would come back to our family room. I'd see the reality of his slowly deteriorating body, and I'd ache for him.

Then one day I heard a song by Twila Paris about a runner. Word by word and note by note, she drew the picture of a person striving to complete a difficult race. Though the contest was long and hard, it was the finish line that brought on the reward. For at the end, the runner ran into his Savior's arms.

Just as my mind had replayed so many of Art's healthy runs, it now picked up Twila Paris's song. Easily, I pictured Art at his running best, cranking out the miles. Only this time, my picture didn't end with the reality of a hospital bed in our family room. This time, my picture ended with the future reality of Art wrapped in the arms of Jesus Christ.

My picture of the future did not erase the reality of our present. It was still hard to see my husband grow weak and eventually even struggle to hold a cup. But when my eyes and heart could not take much more of reality, I'd let my mind jump ahead in time. I'd once again see Art running. I'd watch as Jesus held open his arms and clasped him into his embrace. Somehow it always took the sting out of the present to know what lay ahead for the man I loved.

"And God will wipe away every tear from their eyes; there shall be no more death, nor sorrow, nor crying; and there shall be no more pain, for the former things have passed away. Then he who sat on the throne said, 'Behold, I make all things new.' And he said to me, 'Write, for these words are true and faithful'" (Rev. 21:4-5, NKJV).

Lord, sometimes eternity seems so far away, lost in the reality of now. Please give those who read this book their own song, their own picture, to remind them of the incredible life yet to come. (DH)

No Easy Answers

"Is God fair?" I muttered, while watching television commercials of robustly healthy seniors—laughing, scuba diving, waving from their snowmobiles.

I was thinking of both my husband and myself. His lifestyle and lifetime had spelled out action, from skiing and rock climbing to fly fishing. My activities had traced a different pattern, one that included writing and speaking and mentoring younger women, plus the great joy of grandmothering ten.

The physical and mental limitations imposed on my husband by his stroke were obvious to all, but my life's sudden change of focus and routine didn't show up much on the outside. In my new role as caregiver I had to move swiftly from what we had planned in our lives to a greatly revised lifestyle. Everything slowed down and revolved around the needs of my husband.

It didn't seem fair—or did it? The book of Jeremiah sheds some light on that question: "'For I know the plans I have for you,' declares the Lord, 'plans to prosper you and not to harm you, plans to give you hope and a future. Then you will call upon me and come and pray to me, and I will listen to you'" (29:11-12).

The concept that trials and suffering can actually bless our lives is a deeply Christian insight that we mostly give only lip-service to in this era. Baseball hero Dave Dravecky wrote in *When You Can't Come Back*,

> In America, Christians pray for the burden of suffering to be lifted from their backs. In the rest of the world, Christians pray for stronger backs so they can bear their suffering.

After my husband's stroke, day by painful day I learned that God *is* fair, even when I don't understand what he is up to, even when circumstances obscure a clear view of both his long-range and his day-by-day plans for us. If you ask me how I learned of God's complete fairness in my life, I can only describe the experience as "coming to see his grace and sovereignty," "going through the slow process of giving up my will to his," and "looking back through the years and noticing how right his ways, his plans, turned out to be." Some circumstances are simply part of living in this imperfect world.

Remembering that the reason my plans and my life have changed is not because God is looking the other way. I rejoice in the truth that the Lord's plans are always for our best.

> *"He causes his sun to rise on the evil and the good, and sends rain on the righteous and the unrighteous"* (Matt. 5:45).

There really are no easy answers in this life, Lord, so I am deeply thankful to know that *you* are the only answer, giving me continual hope for a good and satisfying future. (LDV)

What Good Is God?

When our daughter-in-law was a new Christian, she often asked my husband for advice. One day, almost beside herself with the trials of being a new step-mother, she came to Richard for help, and he said, "Painful as it is, God doesn't always give us what we want."

One of the things I love about our daughter-in-law is her honesty and di-rectness. She stammered, "But then, what good is God?"

The truth seems obvious. With my knowledge of the Bible and my rea-soning, I can say God is the source of all the good there is. Nevertheless, when I watched my gentle, generous mother suffer prolonged helplessness, confu-sion, and frequent pain, I cried out, "Why, God?" Asking that, I was in fact ask-ing, "What good is God?"

Ruben Gonzalez knows one answer to that question. He killed a teenager while driving drunk and was sentenced to twenty months in prison. He was a single parent; the sentence would take him from his five-year-old son, who was dying of an inoperable heart condition. Distraught with grief, Ruben ap-pealed his sentence.

His appeal was denied, however, after a counter appeal from the parents of the boy he had killed. In the court room, the angry mother said, "I'm sorry for your son, but if you lose him, you will know something of my pain." Ruben had no hope of relief from his grief and guilt.

And yet, the next day he was called back to court. This same mother had called the judge and asked that Ruben be allowed to remain free as long as his son lived. In the court room she came to Ruben and said, "I want you to know I forgive you." He felt it was a miracle of God, and it was. The mother finally had given her pain and her rage to God.

What good is God? When we give him our pain, he empowers us with his amazing love.

> *"I pray . . . that the eyes of your heart may be enlightened . . . that you may know the hope to which he has called you . . . and his incomparably great power for us who believe" (Eph. 1:18-19).*

Dear God, you and you alone can give peace and hope to my troubled heart and mind. You are the only good I know. I repent of my justified anger, and I repent of my unjustified and unacknowledged anger. Please renew me just as wonderfully as you renewed that broken-hearted mother. (EL)

Wrong Words, Right Heart

As caregivers, it seems we're forever in a vulnerable state. Whether we're coping with the shock of life-changing news or dealing with the load of double work, we tend to be constantly tired emotionally, mentally, or physically.

In our vulnerability, we often hear the wrong words from a friend or family member. Maybe it's a verse quoted one too many times. Maybe it's another story beginning, "Five years ago my aunt had . . ." Or maybe it's advice that digs at the quality of our caregiving. Whatever the words, we're left feeling upset, hurt, or angry.

I felt all of the above when I got off the phone with one friend. She had called to offer sympathy about Art's cancer but ended up saying, "It's really sad that you won't consider taking your husband to the special healing service downtown."

My friend's words put me on the defensive. My mind started replaying our conversation, and I imagined a dozen angry answers. Then doubts began mingling with my anger. Should I try one more thing? When I asked Art about the service, he had said, "Our church elders have laid hands on me and prayed; God is not limited to where he can heal." Even so, should I insist we go?

For the rest of the afternoon I battled emotions that had already been stretched thin by my husband's cancer. Finally, while doing the dinner dishes, I broke down. *Oh Lord, I'm so mad at her. She robbed me of the peace I'd finally begun to feel. Why did she say it? What am I supposed to do now?*

Having spent my meager energy reserves, I finished the dishes in almost a numb state. But in those quiet moments a question came to my mind. *Will*

Satan get one more victory?

The question brought back a plea I'd made to God when the utter reality of Art's cancer replaced my "this must be a dream" feeling. How I hated Satan at that moment, hated his use of this cursed earth for his evil intentions. I begged God, *Don't let Satan get even one more victory in this! He's got Art's body, but please, Lord, nothing else.*

My anger toward my friend lessened as I realized that bitterness would give Satan another triumph. I asked God to help me forgive. I asked him "to let me see my friend's well-intended heart, not just her hurtful words."

My prayer wasn't a new one. After three friends had said all the wrong words to Job, God told him to pray for them. He did, and God richly blessed him. As caregivers, we're blessed with peace when we give faulty words to God and let him transform them into a glimpse of the heart.

> *"After Job had prayed for his friends, the Lord made him prosperous again and gave him twice as much as he had before" (Job 42:10).*

Lord, take the words that hurt, and let me see the heart behind them. Don't let Satan get one more victory because of my anger or bitterness. (DH)

Why Does It Hurt?

At times it seems that illness can tear a family apart. After Lee's Alzheimer's di-agnosis, one of my sons—who had been told all his life how much he was like his father—set out to "punish" his dad for getting sick. He accused Lee of get-ting sick on purpose and was very rude to him. Then he turned his anger on me. I didn't understand that this type of behavior can be normal when a family member is disabled. Then I talked to Milly.

When her parents became disabled, Milly chose to have them move in with her and take care of them herself because her brothers and sisters had children at home. What she wasn't prepared for was the anger she got from those siblings. While growing up, the family had been close; now they were all fighting and arguing over the care of her parents.

While Milly felt it was a privilege to care for her parents, she did not un-derstand her siblings' reactions. They refused to help in the caregiving. They accused her of making the wrong decisions and wouldn't listen to explana-tions from her or the doctor.

As Milly cried out, *Lord, Why does it hurt?* she turned to the Psalms for help. She read them over and over, searching for and receiving comfort. When she read that God punishes those who hurt us, she begged God not to hurt her family. She loved them despite what they had said and done.

We each need to look at the pain behind the anger of our family. When we do this, their attitudes and actions toward us won't hurt as much. We need to remember that their anger really is directed at the disease. Then we can pray that the Lord will heal their hurts as well as ours.

"Bear with each other and forgive whatever grievances you may have against one another. Forgive as the Lord forgave you" (Col. 3:13).

Heavenly Father, thank you for helping me understand that sometimes fear and anger may be the only way my loved ones deal with the losses caused by devastating illness. Give me strength to avoid taking their insults personally and instead to pray more for them. (MAM)

Impossible Prayers

As a caregiver, there were many times I couldn't pray. Sometimes I wouldn't know what to ask from the Lord anymore. I'd prayed and prayed. What else could I say? At other times fatigue and stress robbed me of the ability to focus. My mind jumped among a dozen thoughts. It seemed I couldn't put together a coherent sentence. And then there were times I just didn't want to pray. I didn't want to talk to the God who allowed this disaster to strike my family.

When the first two "I can't pray" situations arose, I took great comfort in knowing that God knew I couldn't pray and that he had promised the Holy Spirit would pray for me. This assurance kept me on my knees, though at times I said nothing and only bowed my head before God. Even when I babbled before the Lord, I believed that the Holy Spirit would sort out my jumbled thoughts.

This promise of the Holy Spirit's help did not encourage me, however, when I didn't want to talk to God because I was angry at him. I didn't always feel angry, but when I avoided talking to God, I knew my heart wasn't feeling love toward him.

Often just realizing that I was avoiding God would send me back down on my knees. But then there were times I didn't care that I was angry. I wasn't going to talk to God and that was that. Somehow, though, I always turned back to him eventually, even if it was only to tell him why I didn't want to talk to him. Like David in many of the Psalms, I'd start off by telling God all the ways that he'd failed my family and me. But then I'd remember something he did—some bit of encouragement he sent or an earlier answer to prayer—and the anger would begin to drain out of me. Word by word I'd come back to the

God who was taking me through my caregiving.

God uses the caregiver's predicament of being unable to pray at times. In some impossible way, he takes our lack of words and turns them into a way to learn more of him. No matter what kind of praying or not praying you're doing today, God hears you.

> *"If we don't know how or what to pray, it doesn't matter. He does our praying in and for us, making prayer out of our wordless sighs, our aching groans" (Rom. 8:26, THE MESSAGE).*

Lord, sometimes it is so hard to talk to you. But hang onto me as you always have, and bring me to my knees before your throne. (DH)

Life in the Slow Lane

My dear neighbor has cared for her disabled husband, Dan, for more than a dozen difficult years. She recently knocked on my door to borrow some laundry soap (caregivers use lots of laundry products!), and she seemed glad to sit and visit for a few minutes. When I asked what she found to be the hardest part of her caregiving duties, Martha lost no time in replying, "I get so tired of 'living slow.'" By that she meant the extra time it took for Dan to eat his food, to get dressed and undressed, to walk and move about with his cane, and, lately, even to remember or process thoughts.

Because Martha was almost always at Dan's side, she felt that her own life was also moving at a snail's pace. "And I worry about the way my frustrations keep building," she added.

Author Ron Davis reminds us, "Emotional wholeness is not a destination. It's a journey. My friend, you and I are on that journey. We are learning, building inner strength, preparing to meet the challenges of the future—and there will be future challenges. In this life we will have trials. . . . It's a natural part of life." (He must have been thinking of Jesus' words in John 16:33: "In this world you will have trouble. But take heart! I have overcome the world.")

Yes, we should take heart when we stop to think what Jesus promises us. And, yes, spiritual growth *is* a daily process that brings about gradual change, increased strength, and greater freedom—freedom in the midst of frustrations and limitations such as halting steps and slowed-down thoughts.

Both Martha and I have found that our burdens seem tolerable when our impatient attitude toward suffering or slowness or any daily trial changes to patient trust in God's sufficiency. Living in the slow lane is not just a burden but a situation God uses to strengthen endurance and increase joy. I think the turning point for me came when I used those slow times to encourage my husband, or to pray for him, instead of clenching my teeth and feeling sorry for myself.

> *"God is our refuge and strength, an ever-present help in trouble. Therefore we will not fear, though the earth give way and the mountains fall into the heart of the sea, though its waters roar and foam and the mountains quake with their surging" (Ps. 46:1-3).*

Sometimes trial works as well as victory, Lord, to shake our souls and let the glory in. A friend told me once that sorrows come to stretch out spaces in our hearts, to make room for the joy. I pray that you will stretch my heart to joyfully include those whose pace is different, those who live in the slow lane. (LDV)

I Don't Want This, God

When my elderly father came home from the hospital, confined for the rest of his life to a wheelchair, his emotional pain was greater than his physical pain. He was a kind man, and I had never seen him enraged and desperate. Now he was. It broke Mom's heart that she could not ease him. I prayed for them, but it seemed that nothing changed. I cried out to God, "I don't want this for my parents!"

To accept the unacceptable, the endlessly painful circumstance, must be done over and over—seventy times seven—like forgiving. Maybe acceptance is another word for forgiving. My parents' unchanging pain hit me daily like a physical blow. I felt I had to turn the other cheek. To whom? To God, who had the power to relieve their suffering and did not. From my limited viewpoint, it seemed so unfair for kind, gentle people to suffer when they were at their weakest—elderly and failing.

Mom had chosen to care for Dad at home, partly because the doctor had said he probably had only four months to live. The months passed until they became years. Dad's emotional distress eased after a few weeks; he gave up his anger and despair and quietly trusted God. Then his physical pain increased; he broke out with shingles. The bathing and dressing of his wounds made more work for Mom. My sisters and I helped as much as we could, but still Mom had most of the load. I grieved for her almost more than for Dad.

I lived an hour's drive from my parents home, and I prayed a lot on my trips to help out. No matter how much I prayed, however, I found no peace. One day I cried out, "It's not fair, God. They're old and fragile, and it just gets harder for them. Why, God? Why?"

Like a clean, cool splash of water, a sentence plopped into my mind. "The earth is the Lord's and the fullness thereof, the world and all they that dwell therein."

What? Was it a Bible verse? It seemed an odd statement with no promise of help, as I had wished. I thought for a minute, replaying the words in my mind: *"The earth is the Lord's"* . . . *I can agree with that. "The fullness thereof"* . . . *yes, all there is in the earth is the Lord's, and he takes care of it, keeps it going. "The world and all they that dwell therein"* . . . *the world is the people. The people are God's also. Does God care about people? Does God care about what's happening to my mom and dad?* I knew he did, and that was why I had been agonizing. Where was God's care?

I can't explain how I could let go of my anger at God, but I think I was impressed that those words had not come from my own mind. They had come from outside of me. Slowly I accepted them as a quiet message from God.

The earth and all who dwell on it are God's business, and, of course, I could not understand the mind of God. I stopped fighting. At last I could accept the humanly unacceptable. A great peace settled over me.

When I got home, I searched in a concordance and found that my message was indeed a Bible verse—Psalm 24:1.

It's been twenty years since God gave that verse to me, and it still calms me. To repeat it to myself is like sailing into a protected harbor in a storm. To know "the earth is the Lord's" gives me peace, courage, and hope.

Perhaps that verse does not hold the same meaning for you, but I hope the way in which I received it may freshen your faith. God is listening. God cares. God communicates.

"My soul finds rest in God alone; my salvation comes from him. He alone is my rock and my salvation; he is my fortress, I will never be shaken" (Ps. 62:1-2).

O Lord God, have mercy on me when I critique your ways. Forgive my foot-dragging and complaining. Enlarge me to fit your gift of love, and ease my aching heart, for you are my loving Father, Father of my Lord Jesus Christ. Thank you. (EL)

Forgiveness

As I learned to care for Lee, at times my emotions got the better of me. Once, on Lee's birthday, I searched the stores trying to come up with something that he would like. I finally found a shirt with fishermen all over it. He used to love to go fishing, so I bought him the shirt.

When I brought it to Lee in the nursing home, however, I didn't get any kind of reaction from him at all. He wasn't even aware there was a present sitting in front of him. I got angry. As I returned to the car, I shoved the tears off my face and slammed the car door as I got in. How dare he not appreciate my shopping for him?

After I calmed down, I was surprised at my reaction. Did I expect that suddenly Lee would be different? Apparently I did. Since he couldn't change, I had to find an answer to how I was feeling, and so I searched the Scriptures.

As I read in Matthew 18, I realized I had never forgiven Lee for deserting me with this illness. Oh, I knew he didn't get this brain disease on purpose, but somewhere in my subconscious I had blamed him for messing up my life, even messing up the joy of shopping for his birthday. It hasn't been easy, but I have asked God to help me forgive Lee. And the next time my emotions try to take over, I hope to be smart enough to search for the reason sooner.

If you feel you need to forgive someone whose illness has hurt you, take a moment and give your anger to God. May you experience, as I did, how wonderful forgiveness feels.

"Be reconciled to God" (2 Cor. 5:20).

Lord, please don't let anger get hold of me again. Show me how to forgive when I need to. Thank you. (MAM)

Escape

One of the hardest things to deal with as a caregiver is not having the freedom to leave the house whenever you want. First, you have to find someone to sit with the disabled family member. Then, you have to make sure the person coming knows if medicine is to be given and when, what to do in an emergency, and who to call if there is a problem.

In my case, Alzheimer's disease trapped me as much as the role of caregiver did. It took away my best friend—my husband. Because I felt trapped, I was angry. "How much longer is this going to go on?" I cried out to God. Perhaps God spoke, but all I heard was silence.

As always, I went to the Bible, the one place where I could find comfort and often answers. In Luke, I was reminded that God took care of the birds each day and that he would also take care of me each day. So I decided to begin each morning by telling myself that with God's help, I could handle that day. I refused to allow myself to think of how many other days I'd already handled or how many more there might be. I could handle today.

I also learned to handle my anger through my writing. I journaled my anger, and I wrote articles that I hoped would one day help some other caregiver who was having the same problems. Some ways I learned to get rid of anger when I could not leave home may help you. They included pulling weeds, taking a fast walk (even around the inside of the house), punching a pillow, and, most importantly, remembering that yes, I could handle one day at a time.

We have already lived through yesterday, and God has not yet given us tomorrow. With God, we *can* handle today.

"For his anger is but for a moment, his favor is for life; weeping may endure for a night, but joy comes in the morning" (Ps. 30:5, NKJV).

Thank you, Father, for reminding me that I am more important than the birds, and just as you take care of them, you will continue to take care of me. (MAM)

Real Questions

No matter how inarticulately we form our questions, they are real. We can't just make them go away because "a good Christian doesn't question God."

I never wanted to doubt what God was doing in my family's life after Art got sick. But at times I couldn't help it. My husband had been an athlete. He ran, fished, backpacked, and rode a bicycle. As his cancer began to take its toll, his muscles wasted away. In time, little more than skin covered his six-foot-plus skeleton. On the days when my eyesight would catch up with what was gradually happening to him, I couldn't help but wonder what God was doing. These thoughts never changed or fixed anything; they just were.

Some time later I was doing a study on the attributes of God. In the introduction the author said something that made me sit up and pay closer attention: "Since the Garden of Eden, Satan's greatest ploy has been to make us question God's character."

Automatically my mind asked, *Is that true?* Flipping my Bible pages to Genesis 3, I reread what Satan said to Eve: "Did God really say, 'You must not eat from any tree in the garden?'" The serpent then said to her, "You will not surely die. . . . For God knows that when you eat of it your eyes will be opened, and you will be like God, knowing good and evil."

Going back over the familiar passage, I realized Satan truly caused Eve to question God's goodness. In his subtle way he told her, "God lied. He didn't tell you not to eat of the fruit for your good, but because he doesn't want you to be like him."

Discovering one of Satan's major ploys didn't make my moments of questioning disappear. But it did help me see what they could become in the enemy's wily hands. That day I purposed to take my questions about God to God.

> *"Don't be deceived, my dear brothers. Every good and perfect gift is from above, coming down from the Father of the heavenly lights, who does not change like shifting shadows"* (James 1:16-17).

Lord, sometimes your love and mercy seem miles away from reality. Yet somehow you always bring me back to the fact that your character is true. You do not lie, and you never allow one tear of pain without purpose. (DH)

Be Angry and Sin Not

Depression often strikes along with a disabling illness or injury. Depression is the anger stage of grief turned inward—frozen anger. When the person we care for is depressed or mentally disabled in some other way, he or she may not be able to express affection or even normal courtesy.

How can we love when we are not loved? In a sermon I've mostly forgotten, my pastor once said, "It's easy to love the lovable, but we are called to love the unlovely."

Brain disabilities and depression can make people lash out in unlovely anger at those they normally love. Unfortunately, my natural reaction to any form of anger is anger, even when I know I'm dealing with a disability. I'd like to lash out myself. During my worst snit fits, I'm helped by Edwin Markham's poem "Outwitted," which I read long ago in grade school. Markham describes someone who had withdrawn from him, retreating within an invisible circle that Markham could not cross. The poet said that with love, he won. He drew a larger circle that took in the angry friend, defenses and all.

I think of Markham's method of conquering with love, and, still angry, I say to myself, "I'll show you! You can't shut me out!" Then I ask God to help me surround the small death of brain disability in my loved one with the vibrant life of Christ's love. The love Christ can give me will be big enough to embrace my depressed loved one, bitterness and all.

In Christ we have a choice: to act or to react. The minute we choose an act of love, the Holy Spirit empowers us. James writes in his epistle, "You do not have, because you do not ask God" (4:2). We can ask to be more loving, and we will receive.

"My command is this: Love each other as I have loved you" (John 15:12).

God, I know anger coming from a brain disability is an illness, but I hurt when I am unjustly accused or treated to angry silence. Please keep my head calm and cool, my heart tender, and grant me more of your love. Thank you! (EL)

The Light Side of Darkness

Few of us can go through the difficulties of caregiving without at some point asking why. For whatever reason, we search for the cause of our circumstances. Inevitably that brings us to God.

My why questions came when I was raising four children alone and my youngest rebelled. After running away from a drug-recovery hospital, she called and asked me to take her back to treatment. When I picked her up, there was a pleading look behind her tear-filled eyes. She said, "Mom, I've done things you could never forgive."

As I assured her of my love and forgiveness, I knew my daughter was at a critical time. To live with her guilt, she needed either to re-find God or harden her heart even more to shut out the pain. As we hugged for the first time in months and my tears dampened her hair, I began praying as never before.

The next day, I asked my church family to fast and pray. Note after note was put in my hand. As they joined me, I fasted, prayed, and begged for my daughter.

When I saw her on the next visiting day, however, I looked into hard eyes and listened to her harsh swear words. Driving home, I couldn't even cry. I could only ask, "Why, God?"

In the privacy of my own bedroom, I began to cry. My thoughts scrambled down a dozen trails trying to explain away my pain—my disillusionment with God. But no matter what I tried, I always came back to the one who controlled all things. In spite of my pleas, he allowed my daughter to harden her heart. My faith faltered. I told God, "If I knew how, I'd give you up."

But I didn't know how.

The next morning I opened my Bible. By "chance" I turned to an account of Israel's history. At the mention of Egypt, I thought of God hardening Pharaoh's heart. I'd never liked that story, but as I read, God brought questions to my mind. *Who would have gotten credit for Israel's release from Egypt, if I had not hardened Pharaoh's heart?*

I guess Pharaoh would have, I answered.

Without the hardness, would he have given a second thought to who the God of Israel was?

No.

Every time I hardened Pharaoh's heart, he came face to face with who I am. By the time his country was destroyed, his son dead, and his army drowned in the Red Sea, he knew he controlled nothing. He knew who I am.

The truth overwhelmed me. Pharaoh had more opportunities to be in heaven because the Lord hardened his heart than if God had never intervened in the Egyptian ruler's life. The hardening of my daughter's heart was not a loss but an opportunity for her to face the Creator of heaven and earth.

God's answer to my why shattered my picture of him and replaced it with an even bigger one. God not only is good; he turns bad into good.

"For the Scripture says to Pharaoh, 'Even for this same purpose I have raised you up, that I might show my power in you, and that my name might be declared in all the earth'" (Rom. 9:17, NKJV).

How easy it is to let circumstances limit you, Lord. Keep me seeing how big my God is. (DH)

My Business . . . or God's?

It's normal and acceptable to feel angry when grief comes. Sometimes however, without realizing it, I cling to anger as a crutch. Rage can distract me from the pain, give me energy, make me feel like I'm accomplishing something. The problem comes when my legitimate anger cools into an attitude and becomes a habit. Then I become self-centered and risk falling into depression—that state of frozen anger.

For me, it's a constant battle to recognize honest anger, deal with it, and send it on its way without hurting anyone, including myself. One person who helps me do this is my friend Annie. She was battered by her biological mother until she was five. Then, after she was adopted, her adoptive father began to molest her. He frightened her into silence by threatening to send her to an orphanage if she ever told anyone.

As a senior in high school Annie moved out on her own. Years later, on the advice of a counselor, she prayed until she could go to her adoptive father and tell him she forgave him. He only said, "Nothing really happened."

Soon after that, her father died, but for Annie that was not the end. Years later she realized that if she saw him in heaven she would not be able to go to him and hug him. She still had not fully forgiven him. She studied her Bible and prayed and wrote in her journal until, she says, "I finally saw that what my father did to me was between him and God. It was not my business. It was God's business. When I accepted this, I could forgive and be free."

In light of what she suffered, her words, "It's not my business," take on a powerful meaning to me. I figure if she can leave her justified rage at God's feet, as I know she has, maybe I can, too. Whenever I don't know what to do with my anger, I remember that maybe justice is not my business.

God's business is to manage justice and vengeance and mercy. He will bless us immeasurably when we can leave his business in his hands.

> *"Praise be to the Lord, for he has heard my cry for mercy. The Lord is my strength and my shield; my heart trusts in him, and I am helped"* (Ps. 28:6-7).

Merciful God, you know I'm staggering along in this world like a blind person, because I can't understand what is happening or why. Nevertheless, I trust you. I know you love me and my loved one and you will redeem and glorify every moment of our suffering in your good way and in your good time. (EL)

Patience

Does the one you care for sometimes find it difficult to recall and verbalize specific words? One morning I found myself getting exasperated over just that kind of situation, but the Lord seemed to stop me in the midst of my frustration—to remind me that he already knows those elusive words, to remind me that as a caregiver I need to be patient and understanding. People who have spiritual strength and assurance can be gentle because they, like God, are strong in a loving desire to help. So it is the gentleness of God which enables us to become patient and understanding.

I often pray for patience with things I cannot control. I'm so filled with egotistic esteem, however, that I still try to manipulate everything to suit my plans. And when the winds and rains don't obey my will, I admit to becoming cross and contrary, despite my good intentions. Then it is back to square one again, back to asking God for needed patience.

Caregiving may involve a bit of conflict, and our basic response is usually to lash out or to find someone else to blame. In *Love Is a Decision,* Gary Smalley and John Trent offer some suggestions that have helped me in these times of difficulty:

- Become soft and tender with the person. By your attitude, nonverbal messages, and voice, tell the person you care about him or her. Sometimes softness alone can open a person's spirit that has been closed by anger, and allow you to get back in harmony with that person.

- Acknowledge that the person is hurting, and be sure to admit any wrong in provoking anger. Admitting we are wrong (when we clearly are) is like drilling a hole in our loved one's "anger bucket" and allowing that unhealthy emotion to drain away.
- Touch the other person gently. Persistent softness—expressed in meaningful touches—can go a long way toward draining anger and negative feelings from a relationship.

At a Bible conference many years ago, a speaker remarked how lovely it was when the strong are also gentle. I've been trying, ever since, to weave the two together! It is so easy to depend only upon our own strength as caregivers, but God brings us back to reality by urging us to follow this Scripture:

"Let us then approach the throne of grace with confidence, so that we may receive mercy and find grace to help us in our time of need" (Heb. 4:16).

Teach me, Father, that some things are beyond my control, and give me the grace to accept those things. Teach me when to advance, when to stand pat, and when to retreat. Lord, teach me patience! (LDV)

God in the Middle

As caregivers, we face a lot of things that are beyond us—beyond our energy, our patience, our endurance, and our understanding. While caring for my mom and dad, I frequently found myself crying out, "Why, God?"

When I have reached my limit, I've often been helped by the insights of others who courageously lived their faith despite suffering. One such person who has always inspired me was a caregiver to many. Dietrich Bonhoeffer, a pastor in Nazi Germany, was imprisoned and ultimately lost his life because he was determined to be a good shepherd to many believers.

In his *Letters from Prison,* Bonhoeffer coined the term, "God's beyond." Of course, nothing is beyond God, so this is really a term to describe *our* "beyond."

In many ways, the responsibilities of caregiving place us in a type of prison too, and also for honorable reasons. Therefore I think carefully about what Bonhoeffer means when he says that God's "beyond" is not the same as our "beyond."

God is always beyond us because he is God, but he lives powerfully with us in what we can understand. The times when I saw my silent prayers soothe Mom and help her sleep peacefully all night, God was as close as my breath. When my sister's prayer with Dad lifted his depression, and he began to read his Bible daily, God was as close as our heartbeats. We had never seen Mom and Dad pray aloud or hold hands in public, so when Mom and Dad reached out for each other and held hands during the prayers of their TV minister, we knew God was as close as our own souls.

Bonhoeffer said, "The church stands, not where human powers give out, on the borders, but in the center of the village." Just so, God lives in the center of our lives even when we are in circumstances beyond our strength, and he shows himself most clearly during our hard times.

If we watch for God's presence and trust him in the midst of our pain, we can leave our outer borders—all of our whys—in his care. Then our "beyond" becomes "God's beyond," and we can find peace.

> *"The Lord is close to the brokenhearted. He saves those whose spirits have been crushed. Come near to God, and God will come near to you"*
> *(Ps. 34:18 and James 4:8,* NCV*).*

Our Father, we want to leave all of our whys in your care. Forgive us when we try to take them back. Help us to focus on all we can understand about you, for this is where we can find all the answers we need. (EL)

Difficult Decisions

At times does a decision you have made leave you feeling guilty? Some decisions might include telling loved ones they can't do what they want to because it is dangerous or impossible for them.

There have been many decisions like that for me. One of the most difficult times was shortly after Lee was diagnosed with Alzheimer's disease. I knew it was no longer safe for Lee to drive, but he refused to stop driving even though he'd had several minor accidents. He had gone to renew his driver's license, and even though he failed the written test, the DMV still renewed his license.

I had to call the DMV and explain the situation. They had me bring Lee back in so they could take him out on the road. Then they took away his license. Lee's anger and frustration only added to my guilt at taking one more step against his independence.

To add to this guilt, I heard several sermons exhorting wives to submit themselves to their husbands. I agreed with this, but when I let Lee make any decisions, they were not logical, so I began to make the decisions without consulting him.

It was a relief to discover other wives who felt these same kinds of feelings. Grace's husband had developed a brain tumor, Mattie's husband had suffered a stroke, and Betty's husband's personality had changed due to a cerebral hemorrhage. Not one of them was able to make logical decisions, and the wives had to take over this role. Each of the women also felt guilty.

Searching for some answers in my Bible, I read in 1 Samuel 25 about Abigail and saw her in a new light. Her husband was probably an alcoholic. Abigail had to learn to step in and do what she felt was the right thing to do. And God not only gave her the wisdom to make the right choices when her husband could not; he also blessed her life.

I learned that God does not expect you or me to force someone who is incapable of making a decision to try to make one anyway. With God's help, we can make the difficult decisions ourselves.

"For I know the thoughts that I think toward you, says the Lord, thoughts of peace and not of evil, to give you a future and a hope" (Jer. 29:11, NKJV).

God, please give me not only the wisdom I need to make any decisions I must make, but also the peace only you can give to go along with those decisions. (MAM)

Antidote for Guilt

My friend Janet has lovingly cared for her mother for several years, but the task has become more demanding in the past six months. When I stopped by her home with some mid-morning refreshment last week, Janet seemed uncharacteristically "down." As we sipped our hot spiced cider and nibbled at the doughnut holes, Janet confessed what was bothering her the most:

> I no longer have a mom. In this reversal of roles she is the child, and I have to be the parent. This seems like such a travesty of our lives, knowing that she will never again be the mother I remember and need. She will always be a prisoner of that horrendous Alzheimer's. Sometimes I cry a lot. Then the guilt feelings engulf me.

I shifted in my chair and recalled words from a book I had recently read, Madeleine L'Engle's *The Summer of the Great Grandmother*. I passed one of L'Engle's thoughts on to Janet: "I must love my mother enough to accept her as she is, now, for as long as this dwindling may take; and I must love her enough, when the time comes, to let her go into a new birth, a new life."

Janet tentatively smiled as she considered the encouragement of someone she didn't even know, someone who shared the same feelings and circumstances which troubled her. Then she abruptly frowned, as she told me of her guilt over the surges of anger, the lips-pressed-together responses to the unpleasant and unremitting chores of caregiving—the cleaning up after chin dribbles and other mealtime spills, the soiled or wet clothing and bedding to handle, the repeated questions to try to answer. Guilt for those feelings was adding an unbearable burden to an already difficult caregiving role.

Together we searched the Bible for the comfort she needed, and Janet wrote out the words of a Psalm as a daily reminder:

> *"What happiness for those whose guilt has been forgiven! What joys when sins are covered over!" (Ps. 32:1, TLB).*

Thanks for teaching me, Lord, that you often comfort us, not by changing the circumstances of our lives (usually our first choice), but by changing our mindset and our attitudes. (LDV)

Not Guilty!

It's surprisingly easy to feel guilty about being strong and well while our loved ones are weak, ill, or disabled. Confusing guilt with sympathy, we may feel it's unloving not to feel guilty. However, feeling guilty about something that is not our fault will not lift the suffering of our loved ones, and it can destroy us.

A few years ago a man walked through Oregon carrying a life-size—or should I say a death-size—wooden cross. Maybe you saw him where you live too. He wanted to walk all over the world, calling attention to the cross of Christ. While I wouldn't belittle the impact of his message, it seemed to me that his energy might have been better spent by helping people in the name of Christ. He might have volunteered to work in a street mission for the homeless or acted as a Big Brother to one fatherless child.

Something about his cross carrying seemed false, despite his obviously good intentions. He reminds me of my friend, who, out of false guilt, snatched up burdens that she really didn't have to carry. After a while she suffered a nervous breakdown, brought on because she was consumed with visiting her mother daily in a nursing home and doing things for her that someone else could do.

While we as caregivers often have to do more than seems humanly possible, it is also our responsibility to be reasonable with ourselves. I believe part of our moral assignment is to set limits and be kind to ourselves so that we can last the course.

When we sacrifice out of love, without any hidden sense of guilt about not deserving to be the survivor, we honor God. Letting false guilt drive us is instead a way to play God. False guilt pushes us beyond what God gives us grace to do. It's as if we feel that what God intends for us to do is simply not enough. False guilt can make us act as if we know better than God. Our Creator designed us with needs of our own and with signals to tell us when to rest and sleep. We are only called to do what we can within God's design for us and to leave the rest to God.

I think King David understood not only true guilt, but false guilt. He said, "Who is aware of his sins? From those that are secret pardon me; from those presumptuous sins too, keep thy servant away: let them not rule over me" (Ps. 19:12-13, BERKELEY).

Whenever I feel like I can't do enough, I search my heart for the lies of false guilt. Is this task really necessary? Who will it help most? Can someone else do it? Is my desire to do this out of the calmness of love or the desperation of false guilt? If I find I'm motivated by desperation, I ask for forgiveness for falling prey to pride—for thinking I know better than my heavenly Father.

The last thing we caregivers need is unnecessary burdens. Learn to recognize and reject false guilt. We are each God's most precious child, whom he freely forgives and sets free from all guilt.

"I write to you, dear children, because your sins are forgiven through Christ" (1 John 2:12, NCV).

Dear heavenly Father, through Jesus Christ you have given me your love and life with you forever. Please grant me one thing more: the wisdom to recognize false guilt and quickly let go of it. Forgive me for snatching up burdens that you never meant for me to bear. (EL)

Looking Grief in the Face

I'd been told not to be surprised if I felt guilt and grief when it was time to put Lee into a nursing home. When I made this decision, all I felt at first was relief. I learned in the next several months, however, that it is dangerous to run away from grief. God gives us grief for a purpose, and, when we refuse to grieve out of fear or some other reason, we can get ourselves into trouble.

After I'd started the paper work for the nursing home, Lee's best friend, Greg, and his wife, Dixie, came for a week's visit. We all had a good time. Lee remembered Greg and responded to him occasionally. I could sense, though, that there was tension between Greg and Dixie. It seemed they were having problems in their marriage. Added to that, I was feeling a strong attraction to Greg.

A few days after they left, I signed Lee into the nursing home. I began to tell myself the depression I felt was because I missed Greg, not because Lee was now in a nursing home. Every time I felt tears near the surface, I ordered myself not to cry. I'd cried enough. When friends from church asked how I was doing, I'd tell them everything was just great.

Whenever my mind turned to Lee and any feelings I might have about our situation, I pushed my thoughts to Greg. At times I felt like the cartoon character with a devil on one shoulder and an angel on the other shoulder. One day I'd pray for Greg and Dixie to work things out, and the next I'd pray for God to work a miracle so Greg could be mine with no one hurt in the process.

I wrote to Dixie and Greg often and spent hours looking at romantic cards I wanted to send Greg but knew I couldn't. I didn't want to hurt Dixie, but I wanted to love and be loved by Greg.

Because it hurt to feel, I became busier than ever. I signed up for more classes then I'd originally planned on taking at the community college. I wrote and studied in the mornings, attended classes from 11:30 to 3:00 in the afternoon, worked from 3:30 to 7:30 in the evening at the college, then visited with Lee. After that, I went home to start my homework plus spend time with my teenagers. Every night I fell into bed exhausted.

I built a wall around my emotions for Lee and, in any spare minutes I had, allowed myself to think only about Greg. I knew that if he lived closer, we were vulnerable for an affair.

Then I read a book, *Who Says Winners Never Lose?* by Diana Kruger. I read that I was *in* the midst of three unhealthy responses to grief. I was suppressing my feelings, replacing what I had lost, and keeping busy. I wanted to throw the book through the window. The author was wrong!

As I read more, the book knocked a chunk out of the wall of my reserve, but still I felt I was right and the book was wrong! I wanted to cry.

Several days later, as I talked on the phone to the editor of a newsletter I wrote for, she asked me to write about how I dealt with putting Lee in a nursing home. As I wrote, more chunks fell out of my invisible wall. The book was right. I was wrong. I told God that I loved Greg. I felt God tell me to pray for Greg and Dixie. I did, but with mixed emotions.

On Thanksgiving, Greg and Dixie called. While I talked to Greg, he told me they had worked things out in their marriage. I felt as if someone had just kicked me in the stomach. Throughout the day I alternated between being glad for Greg and Dixie and angry at God because Greg couldn't be mine. After several hours of this emotional roller coaster ride, I accepted that Greg belonged with Dixie. For the first time in months the tears came. I had to accept that no matter how many times I'd already gone through the grief process with Lee's disease, I wasn't finished.

That Thanksgiving was when the grief process started—again. It took longer to go through because I'd shoved it aside for so long. God sent the tears to help heal the pain; he was also the one to wipe them away; even more important, he helped me to get through the biggest temptation I've ever had to face. God triumphed.

"He will swallow up death forever. The Sovereign Lord will wipe away the tears from all faces" (Isa. 25:8).

Dear Father, thank you for your faithfulness to me. (MAM)

Happiness

As a child, I believed in "happily ever after." I had read all the fairy tales. I'd watched the TV programs in which everything worked out OK in thirty minutes to an hour. I was sure this was the way life was supposed to be. Even after my first husband left me with a six-month-old infant, I was convinced that most husbands were knights in shining armor just waiting to meet all my needs. For the next twelve years, I dreamed of this Prince Charming who would come along and sweep me off my feet and supply all my wants and needs, just as I was positive my father had done for my mother.

Lee did bring great joy into my life, but I learned fast that my version of "happily ever after" was fantasy. When he was diagnosed with Alzheimer's, I had to face what seemed like a total loss. I had to learn that happiness did not depend on my husband, my children, or anyone else. Happiness depends solely on me and my relationship with God.

Daily, I had to ask God to change not only my thinking, but also me. I had to ask him to take away the negative thoughts. And I saw that he began to fill me with his love and his spirit. Now I know that God is the only perfect someone we will ever have in our lives.

We caregivers may not have the fairy tale life we once dreamed of, but we can have the most important thing there is—Christ and his salvation and love. In Christ we know that we will have the one true "happily ever after"—with him.

"The Lord is my strength and my song; he has become my salvation" (Ps. 118:14).

Lord, help me to show others that your love is more important than the love of an earthly spouse or even of my children. (MAM)

Seeing Past Guilt

You lose your temper with your mentally challenged daughter. You feel resentment toward your disabled spouse. You wish your elderly parent would quit hanging on to life. Each of these incidents and dozens more like them can bring a rush of guilt and remorse. You quickly ask God to forgive you, but the next day it comes again.

Guilt and the effort to free ourselves from it can set up a vicious cycle for the caregiver. I got caught in it when I had to set limits on what I would do for my husband. The entire fourteen years of our marriage he had been the head of our home, but gradually his requests became physically taxing and irrational, even though his voice sounded normal. Regularly I fought guilt battles when I told him no, or when I said yes but felt angry about it, or even wished him dead so it would all be over.

I wish I could say that I found a once-for-all solution to my guilt, but I did not. Instead God helped me see ways to deal with it. Sometimes I'd talk about my guilt with people who loved my husband, such as his parents. They were often the objective voice I needed to silence my nagging guilt.

At another time, God used guilt to force me to take a much-needed break. I had begun to hope that Art would die, and my feelings horrified me. I'd ask God to forgive me over and over, trying to rid myself of my awful thoughts, but from time to time they resurfaced. Finally I admitted my thoughts to a friend. She said, "Debbie, you need to get away for the day. Nothing will seem quite as bad when you come back." She was right.

At still other times it made a huge difference to simply talk to God about my struggle. One day I was pouring out my frustration mingled with guilt and this thought came to my mind, *Your guilt shows that you are not hardened. It shows I am still helping you through this. I am keeping you tender and sensitive.*

Each of these things helped me deal with the guilt I felt as I gave Art the care he needed. Looking back, I see where even guilt had a purpose.

> *"You, who have shown me great and severe troubles, shall revive me again, and bring me up again from the depths of the earth. You shall increase my greatness, and comfort me on every side"* (Ps. 71:20-21, NKJV).

Lord, sometimes guilt just won't leave me alone. I need relief. Please open my eyes and help me see how to deal with it. (DH)

He Will Forgive

In the frustration of being a caregiver we've probably all done something we've regretted. I remember one such incident before Lee's diagnosis when he was being totally illogical. I had not yet learned that you cannot reason with someone who has Alzheimer's disease and is thinking illogically.

We were out driving one Saturday looking for yard sales when Lee slammed on the car brakes because he wanted the man behind us to hit us. The man became angry, of course, and Lee couldn't understand why I was upset.

I refused to let him take the kids anywhere in the car until he apologized, and Lee refused to apologize for something he didn't see was wrong. As the week went by, we fought about it constantly. Then one night right before dinner, I got so upset I punched Lee on the arm. He just looked at me and turned and walked away. I fell apart in tears. What had I done?

Long after the disease had caused Lee to forget the incident, it would haunt me. I couldn't forgive myself for what I had done.

Then I began to look up verses on forgiveness. I learned and soon accepted that when I asked God for his forgiveness, he gave it to me. God would also forget what I had done, not because he has Alzheimer's disease, but because he loves me enough to forgive and forget my sins. There were other times when my frustration caused me to sin, but I learned to go immediately to God for forgiveness, which he always granted.

God always forgives when we turn to him, for he understands our frustration. Besides going to God with your frustration, try journaling your emotions. Sometimes getting it out on paper (or a computer screen) will help you to understand yourself. Whether or not you journal, remember that God always understands what we are feeling.

> *"If we confess our sins, he is faithful and just and will forgive us our sins and purify us from all unrighteousness"* (1 John 1:9).

Father, thank you for forgiving my sin—even the sins caused by my frustration at the disease. (MAM)

The Value of Our Best

When a person takes on caring for another, a lot of other things in life get put on hold: church ministry, volunteer work, classes—many activities that provide pleasure and fulfillment. At first it is simply a necessary part of our life-changing adjustment, but as time passes it can become a personal void. Somehow changing sheets and cooking special foods doesn't seem to make the most of a person's abilities and gifts.

When my husband got sick, I was teaching a women's Bible study and a Sunday school class and volunteering in my children's classes at their school. Each of these pursuits had to be given up. Without these outlets in my life, I began to wonder if my brain wasn't fermenting in the laundry basket. Then I read a parable by Lettie Cowan in *Streams in the Desert*. It went like this:

A king once went into his garden and found everything withered and dying. He asked the oak tree that stood by the gate what the trouble was. The oak answered, "I am sick of life because I am not tall and beautiful like the pine."

The pine tree was out of heart too because he could not bear grapes like the vine. The vine wanted to wither away because it could not stand erect. The geranium fretted because it wasn't fragrant like the lilac. And so it went throughout the garden.

But then the king came to a little heartsease and found it bright, healthy and cheerful. The king said, "Well, heartsease, I'm glad, amidst all this discouragement, to find one brave little flower. You do not seem to be discouraged like the others."

The little flower replied, "No. I know I'm not of much account, but I thought that if you wanted an oak, pine, vine or lilac, you would have planted one here. But instead you planted me, so I know you wanted a heartsease, and I am determined to be the best little heartsease that I can."

Reading this story made me realize that for now, God did not want me to be a Sunday school teacher, Bible study leader, or school volunteer. He wanted me to be a caregiver, and so the task deserved my best efforts. It was a divine appointment.

"And whatever you do in word or deed, do all in the name of the Lord Jesus, giving thanks to God the Father through him" (Col. 3:17, NKJV).

Lord, being a caregiver isn't glamorous. Many of its tasks are menial. But always help me remember it is a job given by and done for the King of kings and Lord of lords. (DH)

Take Forgiveness

Guilt is an occupational hazard for caregivers. We catch it like a virus. The conditions that make each of us susceptible are as different as we are from each other, and as common as our caregiving situations. Feeling guilty can be like a fever—a warning that we need care.

For me, the most difficult type of guilt is often *hidden guilt*—I'm so ashamed of some of my thoughts and attitudes, I don't want to admit them. So I go around with a case of what I call "walking pneumonia of the spirit."

Here's where the infection hits me. I love myself best. I hate being under the authority of someone else, even God. I want to do my own thing. I get really angry when someone encroaches on my rights. Then there's the family of fear bugs. I don't trust God. His ultimate plan for me may be gloriously good, but what will he ask me to suffer to get there?

Walking pneumonia of the spirit is deadly for caregivers. But thank God it's not only treatable, but curable.

The Lord fights the infection for me. At the times I can best understand, he shows me the consequences of my hidden sins, so I can see the need for his prescription—a good dose of repentance. He forgives me and helps me to change my way to his way. As Soren Kierkegaard said in *Journals,* "God creates out of nothing. Wonderful, you say. Yes, to be sure, but he does what is still more wonderful: He makes saints out of sinners." How glad I am that God works this wonder in my life. He forgives, heals, and strengthens me against new infections.

This type of guilt—the kind that makes me recognize my sin and brings me to confession—is a painful, exhausting dis-ease, so it must be taken most seriously. Watch for early symptoms, search out smoldering infections, and call the Great Physician right away. Then take his forgiveness morning and night and as often as needed in between.

"Happy is the person whose sins are forgiven, whose wrongs are pardoned" (Ps. 32:1, NCV).

I love this prayer; it says all I want to pray and sometimes by myself forget to say: "Forgive me my sins, O Lord; forgive me the sins of my youth and the sins of mine age, the sins of my soul, and the sins of my body, my secret and whispering sins, my presumptuous and crying sins, the sins that I have done to please myself, and the sins that I have done to please others. Forgive me those sins which I know, and those sins which I know not; forgive them, O Lord, forgive them all of thy great goodness." *1560 prayer book "Private Devotions"* (EL)

Am I a Victim?

Do you ever feel you've had more than your fair share of trouble? Things go wrong, one problem piling upon another, until the worst possible thing happens at the worst possible time. "Murphy's law!" we say, and try to laugh. But sometimes, it hurts too much to laugh. We feel like a victim with no victim's rights.

The truth is, however, that God didn't design us to accept the role of victim. He gave us the power to choose our attitude, if not our circumstances.

Some courageous nuns showed me how much can be endured without becoming a victim. In Africa during one of the bloody revolutions for independence from European domination, when rebel gangs roamed and killed randomly, nuns in a mission hospital were taken prisoners. They were repeatedly raped as the rebels dragged them across the continent. One young nun felt so defiled and degraded, she became suicidal.

An older nun, who suffered the same treatment, begged the younger woman to remember that they were the brides of Christ, and that because they lived with their lives hidden in him, no one could really defile them. Clinging to this mysterious truth of our faith, the young woman regained her balance. Both nuns survived the ordeal with their spirits and minds whole.

When we remember who we are in Christ, no one can make us victims. Sometimes I forget this and play the poor-me game. And then I remember the nuns. No person and no circumstance can make us victims without our consent. Only we have the power to make ourselves victims. We have the freedom to choose.

"No, in all these things we are more than conquerors through him who loved us"
(Rom. 8:37).

Our Father, you made me but a little lower than the angels. You created me to become your own child! Remind me of who I am when I'm tempted to accept the role of victim. In Christ I am a victor, not a victim! Amen! (EL)

A Break for Love's Sake

"You need to get away and have some time to yourself."

This standard advice to caregivers is usually easier said than done. Friends can come over only so often. Money for hired help only stretches so far. And the person you're caring for can endure only so much change and shifting around. But these difficulties pale when compared with the guilt caregivers can feel when they start taking steps to meet their own needs.

Thoughts about being selfish or not loving enough tend to prick at the caregiver, making the idea of getting away a muddle of relief and misery. This muddle kept me from taking regular breaks for a long time. I had to realize that the love and selflessness I kept trying so desperately to preserve was threatened most by my not caring for myself. The day-after-day giving without relief was beginning to cause tentacles of resentment, self-pity, and even anger to wrap around my heart.

It came to a head one night as I scrubbed the carpet next to Art's bed for the third time that day. As I paused to push aside the pile of soiled linens and pajamas, total exhaustion brought me to a breaking point. I wanted to shout at Art and chuck the dirty wash into the trash. I stopped scrubbing and started crying.

Art sat in a chair near me, and I ended up laying my head on his lap. I told him how I was feeling, and he said he understood. But as soon as my tears dried, he said, "Could you bring me a cup of hot tea?"

In utter frustration, I got up and headed toward the kitchen. Art's non-stop drinking was what caused the continual messes. Turning the stove on under the kettle, I was struck by the irony of the situation, and I ended up laughing, largely in emotional release.

Art's inability to eat was causing him to starve, producing an electrolyte imbalance that affected his brain. It allowed him to talk rationally but not to understand. If I got help, it would have to be my decision. The next day, I called my medical insurance company to find out what respite benefits I had. I called some close friends to ask for help. And I called a local nursing firm for care prices. In the end I established a pattern of getting away for two afternoons a week, one by myself and one with our children.

Sometimes, walking out the door, I felt intense relief, and sometimes, intense guilt. Sometimes I came home refreshed and ready to go; other times I didn't want to have to return. But as the months passed, my afternoons away from caregiving allowed me to keep my deep love for Art to the end of his life.

"After he had dismissed them, he went up on a mountainside by himself to pray. When evening came, he was there alone" (Matt. 14:23).

Lord, it can feel so selfish getting away; it can feel so difficult coming back. But better than anyone, you understand we are just dust. Somehow use our away times to keep us healthy, to keep us loving. (DH)

No Time for Myself

Often those who need round-the-clock care are senior citizens—people for whom time takes on a different rhythm. Sometimes we grow impatient with their unhurried pace and preoccupation with the past. We want more time for our own interests.

As my friend Norma and I worked in our church nursery recently, cuddling and changing babies, she related the highlights of her eightieth birthday the previous week. She also confided that when she was young the days seemed plentiful and cheap. Like penny candy, she seemed to always have a pocketful, which she spent casually. "Now," she observed, "my supply of time has diminished, and the value of each day has soared like the national debt. Suddenly I find myself cherishing, even hoarding, the hours."

For both caregiver and the one being cared for, God has some incredible promises. One of my favorites is: "The righteous will flourish like a palm tree. . . . They will still bear fruit in old age, they will stay fresh and green, proclaiming, 'The Lord is upright; he is my Rock'" (Ps. 92:12, 14-15).

We hear about growing old gracefully, but I suspect that our heavenly Father wants all of his children also to grow old *gratefully*. God wants me to live as though he were listening and talking to me in each day's circumstances. That way I'm enabled to praise him for the small things I might otherwise overlook, as well as for major matters—such as my eternal life in Christ. With this perspective my reserves of available time seem to stretch, too, to meet the day's demands.

You might want to join me in pursuing a grateful-to-God mindset, so that from now through our older years, we truly age gracefully, and so that our own hours and months now as caregiver and as child of God will be refreshed by him.

> *"Therefore, since we are receiving a kingdom that cannot be shaken, let us be thankful, and so worship God acceptably with reverence and awe"* (Heb. 12:28).

Give me understanding, Lord, of the different perceptions we all have of time. As a caregiver may I be willing to take the time to minister compassionately as you did when you were here on earth. And give me, I pray, a grateful heart, as I focus on all that I have from you rather than on what I think I lack. (LDV)

Healing

With the situations we caregivers must deal with, the patterns of our lives change. Holidays change; so does our social life. We may sometimes feel like Humpty Dumpty—broken and forgotten. But change does not have to mean wreckage. We can heal. We can be mended. To do so, I've learned to pay attention to the basics.

I saturate my life with the Bible. I go to God when the pain becomes too much to bear. I have learned to let myself cry. I've learned to laugh again. I journal when I am hurting.

Life's basics include proper food for the body, exercise, and sleep. On nights when my mind won't shut down and I can't go to sleep, I try to remember all the Scripture I have memorized starting from *A* and going to *Z*. Then, if I'm still awake, I pray.

I try to find pleasure in simple things: clouds that make pictures, a lightning storm, the laughter of a child. Most important, I find pleasure in knowing Christ loves me. He will not desert me because of illness, his busy schedule, or anything else. God promised in the Old Testament that he would be a husband to the widow and a father to the fatherless. I believe that includes all of us, and we can hold on to this promise daily.

One way to remember God's promises is to put up cards where you can read them, some in your house and some in your car. At times, one word is all it takes to remind us of what we can do to help our healing process. That word might be *smile, sing, journal,* or *rest*. Use any words that will remind you to pay attention to your own needs as well as the needs of the one you care for.

"No longer will they call you Deserted" (Isa. 62:4).

Dear Father, I thank you that you will remain with me always. I thank you for the little blessings you send my way each day. Help me to always look for them. (MAM)

Bringing Dreams to God's Altar

A hard moment in caregiving comes when you realize your plans and dreams for the future are, at best, postponed and, at worst, lost. This realization often doesn't hit hard at first. It is the least of your concerns as you face the immediate crisis that flips your world upside-down and turns you into a caregiver.

But eventually your mind thinks about what you had planned or dreamed. Eventually you realize these things are not going to happen as hoped. Some of your plans were conscious, such as seeing a child go on to college or traveling with your spouse someday when the kids left home or hosting big family dinners on the holidays. Others were unconscious, such as having a healthy child or having grandparents your children could spend a week with or always sharing family responsibilities with a spouse.

With the reality of lost dreams comes grief. I started grieving for our lost future when Art was nine months into his cancer. New tumors had brought a terminal diagnosis, and his failing health meant more caregiving. Somewhere in the middle of this increasing need for care, I realized that Art and I would never have our time alone. We'd married in college and decided to start our family as soon as Art graduated. We had our four children quickly, and, to console ourselves when it appeared there would never be an end to diapers, we'd talked of how all the kids would be grown and gone when we were forty-five years old. We'd have our time together then, enjoying adult relationships with our kids and freedom from child care.

But Art would never see his thirty-sixth birthday. If I traveled, I'd do it alone. If we had grandchildren, I'd enjoy them alone. And when future holidays came, I'd wait for our grown children alone.

My thoughts left me depressed and full of self-pity. Not wanting to lay another burden on Art, I took my grief to God, half angry and half wanting a miracle to "fix it." Instead, God whispered into my thoughts, "Put your dreams and plans on the altar of sacrifice to me."

To help me do the impossible, I pictured myself laying all our plans on an altar of stone. In my mind I saw fire rise up and consume them. The smoke from their demise lifted into heaven. Even as I watched my half-imagined and half-real sacrifice, God reminded me that to him it had a priceless aroma.

"[It is] a sweet-smelling aroma, an acceptable sacrifice, well pleasing to God" (Phil. 4:18, NKJV).

Lord, our futures have always been yours, though we made plans for them. Help us give them back to you at this time when we must trust you with our tomorrows. (DH)

The Resentment Trap

I don't suppose many of us had an ambition to be a long-term caregiver. I know I didn't. When it came to caring for my grandchildren in addition to caring for my mother, I resented the task. I didn't know these two children, and they didn't know me. I was angry at their mother for leaving them and found myself resenting the intrusion on my already busy life of the children she hadn't trained right.

I didn't want to resent little people who were so in need, especially my own grandchildren, but I found myself walking around with a chronic disagreeable feeling that I didn't want to admit to anyone but God. I prayed a lot for the ability to lavish love and acceptance on Jennifer and Jeff. And yet, inside, I couldn't seem to get rid of a lump of irritation and self-pity.

One day, months after the children had moved in, when Jennifer was four and Jeff was two, I promised to take them to the park to play on the swings after I finished some kitchen chores. I told them what I had to do and how long it would take, because Jennifer could tell time. Still, she kept coming to the kitchen door to nag.

"Is it almost time to go?"

"Not yet. Remember what I told you."

A few minutes later, "Can we go now?" She was so excited about going, she was almost dancing.

I replied patiently and told her not to ask again. She tried to be good, but soon returned with the same question. I stayed patient until about the fourth time, and then I thought, *If this were my child, I'd be yelling by now, and that's what I feel like doing.* I straightened up from putting something in the refrigerator and turned to scold her.

As I looked down, I saw a line on the floor between us where the carpet of the dining room met the linoleum in the kitchen. Instantly, I heard a quiet message in my mind: *Whose side are you on—yours or hers? Are you for her or against her?*

Oh, Lord, I'm on her side! I'm for her! I cried in my heart as Jennifer stared up at me with big eyes that were beginning to look worried. In a flood, I could feel again how it is when you are not much more than three feet tall and always have to rely on big people for decisions, and for love.

I smiled and said, "Yes! Get your coat. It's time to go!"

From that moment on, I had a lethal weapon against resentment. I would remember Jennifer's big eyes looking up at me and, below her upturned face, the line on the floor between us. I thank God for whispering that question to me at just the right moment. It has helped me to remember I'm really on the side of the person I'm caring for, no matter how I feel.

Resentment comes because we're tired. It's nearly always a signal to arrange for respite care, to get out of the house and do something enjoyable, and to get more rest. Only by respecting the needs of our own bodies can we stay faithfully on the side of our dependent loved ones. When we do what we can, God will supply what we can't, because he's on our side too.

"Practice living by the Spirit and then by no means will you gratify the cravings of your lower nature. . . . But the product of the Spirit is love, joy, peace, patience, kindness, goodness, faithfulness, gentleness, self-control. . . . Let us walk where the Spirit leads" (Gal. 5:16, 22, 25, WILLIAMS).

O God most high, I know you created me to become a loving person. Thank you for not expecting me to express love on my own! Through your Son you show me how and provide a way. Thank you for washing away my resentments and for filling me with your loving Spirit. (EL)

Loving the Caregiving

Countless times I have complained about the everyday jobs that being a caregiver brings.

Vi's husband, Robert, was disabled from diabetes and heart problems. Every day she had to get into the tub to lift him in and out to bathe him because he only had one leg. After a while this became too difficult for Vi to handle. It became necessary for her to give Robert a sponge bath on the bed every evening after she came home from work.

Vi did this daily just like she did the dishes daily, but she had no joy in the chore. This changed one night, though, when Robert thanked her and told her this was his favorite time of day. Vi's attitude totally changed. She thanked God she could show Robert her love in this daily task, and it became the best time of day for her as well.

There are negative sides to everything we do, including taking care of our loved ones, but we can ask God to give us the power to overcome the negative and look for the positive in every situation. It helps to remember how Jesus washed the feet of his disciples. I have learned to praise God for the chance to follow his example. Jesus lovingly chose to serve others. And Christ even willingly laid down his life for us. Wouldn't it be better to praise God, instead of complaining, when we are asked to give our lives to take care of our loved ones?

"Truly I tell you, just as you did it to one of the least of these who are members of my family, you did it to me" (Matt. 25:40, NRSV).

God, help me to change my attitude and do my caregiving chores with love. (MAM)

Wings of Eagles

As a caregiver, have you ever felt trapped? Before Lee became disabled, he was in the reserves and would often be gone for the weekend or for two weeks at a time. A couple of these times, I didn't have a car and couldn't get out of the house even when I desperately wanted to. That is how I felt after I took care of Lee at home for several years. Most of that time he could not be left alone. Five children at home—four of whom were teenagers—and the day-to-day hassles of parenting and caring for someone with Alzheimer's disease made me feel trapped.

At one time, I went into depression. I wanted to be free to live my own life, not the life of a caregiver that I'd never asked for. I couldn't function.

I remember one day I decided to force myself to write, but when I went to type an envelope to mail the manuscript, I discovered it was just too much trouble to pick up the typewriter. I sat and just stared at the walls for hours. Writing had saved my sanity for several years, but now it was impossible to write. Everything had been drained from me.

In the silence of not being able to function, I began to wait on the Lord. I read Scripture again and again and prayed. Then I received a phone call from someone at church who asked me if I would be willing to talk with a woman who had just found out her husband had Alzheimer's disease. Could I offer her some comfort?

I agreed to try, and as I talked with the woman, it felt good to be able to understand how she felt. Suddenly I realized she probably understood how I felt as well. More important, God understood. With this awareness came a new strength to deal with my own situation again. My ability to write came back. I realized that as long as I thought only of myself, my situation would seem too difficult to handle. When I thought of others, and when I allowed God to use me to help them, God lifted me out of the depression and renewed my spirit. I no longer felt the need to run away.

Don't let yourself feel trapped. God has given us so many ways to renew our spirit. One of the best, I believe, is helping someone else who is in the same situation as we are.

"But those who wait on the Lord shall renew their strength; they shall mount up with wings like eagles, they shall run and not be weary, they shall walk and not faint" (Isa.40:31, NKJV).

Thank you, Father, that when I look away from myself and see others, you lift me up and give me hope. (MAM)

The Relief of Change

As caregivers, we go through a lot of different feelings—grief, fear, denial, anger, depression, hope. When each one comes, it dominates our life, and we have difficulty seeing beyond it.

For me, the worst feeling I went through was what I called the "dark cloud" stage, a time when the worst storms of emotions were over, but I felt as if a huge gray cloud lingered behind. I didn't cry anymore, but I felt no joy either. The worst of my fear and anger had passed, but they weren't gone. Hope wasn't lost now, but neither was it present. I could function efficiently and talk normally, but I merely went through the motions. I felt no spark of real living.

It got so I longed for a good cry, anything besides the day in and day out gray. Surely a storm of tears would wash it away? But songs, sympathy, prayers, stories, old memories—nothing triggered the release of this bleak time. So I just kept on.

I don't know when the dark cloud stage ended. I have no magic moment or specific incident that broke through its heaviness on my life. One day, however, I laughed instead of simply smiling at a funny joke. Another day I noticed the delicious smell of my baking cinnamon rolls. And one morning when I read the Bible, I found myself seeing a great insight. Then a friend invited me to lunch, and I realized that I really wanted to go, even though I had to make special arrangements.

Bit by bit, my dark cloud went away. I cried. I laughed. I felt joy again.

Some time later, I realized that this stage and every other one came and went. It caused me to write in my journal: "Emotions are real. They affect me deeply. But they do not last! They change. No matter how intense they are, THEY WILL PASS."

"Weeping may endure for a night, but joy comes in the morning" (Ps. 30:5, NKJV).

Lord, my feelings are so real to me. But please remind me that they always, always change. Only you never change. (DH)

I Will Trust in God

At times I wanted just to run away from my caregiving situation and get on with my life. Then I met Vic and Deb, a couple whose struggles helped change my perspective.

Vic and Deb were in their thirties when Deb had a stroke. The stroke left her with the mind of a three-year-old child. Vic was devastated. In his grief, he avoided home whenever possible. While he still attended church on Sundays, Vic began to visit bars and drink during the week.

Soon Vic began to see a woman who pushed him to get a divorce. Vic decided to make his wife a ward of the state and get on with his life. But he had no peace about his decision.

One day a friend pointed out to Vic that there are all kinds of ways to do things, but God's way is the best way. Vic began to have doubts about his decision to divorce his wife. In the meantime, Deb was slowly relearning how to do things. Vic became encouraged even though the progress she made was slow.

Emerging from his confusion, Vic finally turned to the Bible for his answer. He found it in two Scriptures: 1 Corinthians 10:13 reminded him that his faithful God would not let him be tempted beyond what he could bear. Proverbs 3:5-6 taught him to acknowledge and trust God.

Today Vic no longer drinks. He has stayed with Deb, and he praises God daily for the slow but steady healing he sees in his wife. Vic is also thankful that they are a testimony not only to God's continued healing of Deb's body, but also to Vic's spiritual healing. And he is thankful for the testimony their healed marriage brings to others.

The thought of divorcing Lee has crossed my mind more than once, especially when I think of all the yesterdays and wonder how many tomorrows there will be. I would also love to get on with my life. But I have chosen to stay married to him. God gives me the strength I need for each day.

When you are sure you can't handle even one more day of being a caregiver, ask God to help you handle today. Through obedience to God and through help from people like Vic whom God puts in our path, we can learn to daily take hold of the strength that God gives us and do things his way.

"Do not be wise in your own eyes; fear the Lord and shun evil" (Prov. 3:7).

Lord, on days when we are tempted to divorce our mates or leave our children because we can no longer deal with the situation, please remind us of people like Deb and Vic. Help us see again the blessings they received as he was willing to do things your way. (MAM)

God's Thirst Quenchers

Caregivers often experience a dryness that is much like our thirsty and dehydrated feelings on a hot summer day. We long for refreshment to ease the brittle edges of our lives. Sometimes it helps me to recall building a snowman last winter with our little granddaughter, or walking at the ocean's edge as water and wet sand tickled my bare toes, or diving into a mountain lake. Sipping an icy glass of lemonade or taking a rejuvenating cold shower are cool things I can actually do. I discovered that the Bible overflows with refreshing passages, ones which demonstrate that God is thinking of more than relief from heat. He wants you and me to be refreshing people!

The apostle Paul frequently praised those who refreshed others by their lives and actions. He commends Philemon by saying, "Your love has given me great joy and encouragement, because you, brother, have refreshed the hearts of the saints" (Philem. 7). Paul also asks the Lord to show mercy to the household of Onesiphorus, because, he writes, "he often refreshed me and was not ashamed of my chains (2 Tim. 1:16). Could God also be reminding me, as a caregiver, to put aside any shame I might try to hide when I am with the one I'm caring for?

According to my dictionary, the word *refresh* means "to revive; to renew by stimulation; to rejuvenate." Many times I've been the recipient of this refreshing kind of ministry. People have refreshed me by saying, "My life is richer because you have . . ." "Your hospitality (music, sewing, Sunday school teaching) is special." This has given me the encouragement I needed to continue on as a caregiver, while also reminding me to refresh others in need.

When we see how the Lord speaks refreshing words to the disciples and the hurting people he encountered, and how Paul in his busy ministry took time to encourage and commend refreshing believers, and when we ourselves experience this touch, it is easy to want to qualify as a "thirst quencher."

"A generous man [or woman] will prosper; he who refreshes others will himself be refreshed" (Prov. 11:25).

Father, thanks for the unexpected gifts of love, no matter what form they take. They refresh my soul and my life so greatly. May I take stock of ways I can be a refreshing person, a breath of fresh air in this weary world. (LDV)

The Extra Mile of Help

For many caregivers, one of the hardest things that they must do is ask for help. It's not so bad at first because friends and family usually offer to lend a hand. But as caregiving becomes a month-after-month job, people tend to get back to their own lives, and the offers of help come less frequently. That's when we can struggle for long periods of time, trying to do everything ourselves.

Maybe it's the admission that our situation is beyond us? Maybe we don't want to bother others or make them feel guilty? Maybe it's our cultural "pull yourself up by your boot straps" pride? Whatever the cause or causes, many of us face real difficulty in picking up the phone and saying, "Can you help me?"

Widowed and left alone to raise four children ages eight through twelve, I found asking for help incredibly hard. In the end, I only asked for assistance when I could pay for it, when a task was beyond me, or when body-aching weariness forced me to.

Today my children are grown, and we share wonderful adult relationships. They appreciate all that I did for them. But in spite of these good things, I've learned that my "do it all, don't ask for help unless desperate" attitude had a price tag. Though I did the right things—drove my kids to practices, attended games, taught them to drive, helped with homework, went on vacations—I look back on few fun memories of these times. Rather than enjoyable experiences, they were never-ending responsibilities, duties.

In my effort to not bother others or to spare my pride by not asking for help, I gave care with little respite until I lost most of the joy of raising my children.

132

Too often we measure the amount of caregiving we can provide by our physical capabilities. But I suggest we measure it by our attitude. When lack of joy, bitterness, anger, or another negative attitude settles in to the point that we are aware of it, it's time to pick up the phone and ask, "Can you help me, today?"

> *"But now indeed there are many members, yet one body. And the eye cannot say to the hand, 'I have no need of you'; nor again the head to the feet, 'I have no need of you.' No, much rather, those members of the body which seem to be weaker are necessary. . . . And if one member suffers, all the members suffer with it; or if one member is honored, all the members rejoice with it. Now you are the body of Christ"* (1 Cor. 12:20-22, 26-27, NKJV).

Lord, it is so hard to ask for help. Even if I do, I often hear a hesitant reply or the words, *Sorry, I can't.* But for the sake of my heart, don't let me give up. (DH)

God's Presence

When I had my husband and five of my children at home, it seemed there were days on end when they all clamored for my attention at once. I remember once when Lee, because of his disease, was being totally illogical, and I was trying to calm him down. At the same time, one of the kids needed to be somewhere, and another wanted to tell me all about her day. Then two of my boys began to argue. I became frazzled—I could have used some attention myself!

Later that night when I was finally in bed, I began to imagine people all over the globe seeking God's attention all at once. How did he handle this?

I knew, of course, that God is able to handle everything all at once, but I decided to search the Bible for those who sought God's attention. In the Gospels there are several incidents in which people sought Jesus. They wanted his attention.

There was the time the woman had been bleeding for twelve years and knew if she could just touch Jesus, he would heal her. She pushed forward in the crowd until she got his attention. In Luke, chapter 5, the friends of a disabled man tore the top of the roof off the house so they could get Jesus' attention.

These people did not give up. They persevered until they had the attention of God.

I discovered that on days when everyone was pressing in on me, I needed to press in on Christ and feel that I had his attention. One way for you to press in on Christ might be to imagine you are reaching for him, but there are all kinds of people around, stopping you. Push your way through the crowd until you can reach his garment. Then relax and just feel his presence.

"The Lord is near to all who call on him" (Ps. 145:18).

God, thank you for being here for me. You are able in your almighty omnipresence to be here for me as well as for everyone else all at once. (MAM)

Breaking Life into Little Pieces

Since becoming a caregiver I've tended to take life more seriously than I used to. I wish laughter came more easily.

Billy Graham writes in *Hope for the Troubled Heart,* "A keen sense of humor helps us to overlook the unbecoming, understand the unconventional, tolerate the unpleasant, overcome the unexpected, and outlast the unbearable." Solomon reminds us that "a happy heart makes the face cheerful" (Prov. 15:13). What an asset a sense of humor is for both caregiver and the one receiving needed help!

Laughter may not come easily in a life with limitations, so we need to be watching for those small moments or incidents that we can turn into a chuckle, a God-provided relief valve. When the pills spill out every which way like rainbow-colored hail on the kitchen floor, just when I'm running late with breakfast; when four-year-old Jessica playfully grabs for Bob's cane at church and runs off with it; when my husband's dangling, inoperative right arm accidently swishes through the butter—these are scenarios with built-in stress potential. However, if I focus on the Lord's promised presence every moment, rather than getting tied up with my own feelings, I can turn such frustrations into a jovial grin. And sometimes I even seem to sense God's enjoyment of the moment also!

In his book *You Gotta Keep Dancin',* Tim Hansel observes: "Humor has the unshakeable ability to break life up into little pieces and make it liveable. Laughter adds richness, texture, and color to otherwise ordinary days. It is a gift, a choice, a discipline, and an art."

A caregiver's cheerful, smiling face may well turn a gloomy, bad-attitude day into one proclaiming God's shining presence and joy—for both me and the ones I love!

"A cheerful look brings joy to the heart, and good news gives health to the bones" (Prov. 15:30).

Help me, dear Lord, to value your gift of laughter, so that joy characterizes each moment of my life. (LDV)

Enjoy God's Beauty

Does the beauty that surrounds you ever become so familiar that you forget it's there? When we first moved to Oregon, I looked out my living room window at the Cascade Mountains and prayed that I would never take this beauty for granted.

Yet, in the midst of caregiving, I forgot to take the time to admire the beauty around me. I remember one particular day. I had taken Lee to daycare, but it was not a day I could rest. My twins were graduating from high school that night, and my parents, who were driving up from California, were to arrive any minute.

I came home after dropping Lee off and tried to rush into the house. Unfortunately, I couldn't get in—my key had broken in the lock. Frustrated, I stormed around the house looking for a way to get in, but everything was locked up tight. I drove over to the high school and got my son out of class so I could get his key.

After I got home, I suddenly stopped and looked around me. It was a beautiful day. It seemed as if the Lord was telling me to just sit outside on the patio and admire the fluffy clouds in the sky and the sunshine peeking out. Then I watched the horse in the field next door as he cantered about. When I finally went into the house, I felt so much better because of my little break. I was then able to thank God that he had forced me to look around and enjoy what he had given me.

Now I take the time to enjoy what God has given me, from the rain to the sunshine, from the hills to the valleys and all the flowers.

"Your works are wonderful, I know that full well" (Ps. 139:14).

Thank you, God, for the beauty you have provided for us. I don't ever want to take it for granted again. (MAM)

Take Heaven

We usually live with less rest and more hurry than our parents and grandparents did. Add caregiving to this and I suspect many of us have forgotten how to really rest.

When I was helping to care for Dad and then later, Mom, it seemed to me that rest was totally out of reach. To get a full night of uninterrupted sleep was so heavenly that when I read Fra Giovanni's insightful words, they made me stop and think—and wish. He said, "No heaven can come to us unless our hearts find rest in it today. Take heaven."

Do I turn away from heaven in my hurrying? Do I blindly race past the outstretched hands of the Lord? Yes, the feeling of being rushed does blind my heart. I think longingly of the time Jesus said to his disciples, "Come away with me and rest."

I want heaven! I need all that heaven means—rest in God's love and the peace of Christ. I need heaven right now, right here. How can I learn to rest in heaven today while I have to keep on working?

My friend Jane has shown me so clearly how an attitude can provide a sense of rest and trust or one of hurry and anxiety. Disabled at birth, Jane suffered nerve damage in her neck and had limited breathing capacity. After numerous childhood surgeries Jane had been able to live a fairly unhampered life. Then, when she reached her fifties, doctors warned her that she would need to be on oxygen in the near future and for the rest of her life.

She absolutely dreaded the thought. Visiting nursing homes had been one of her ministries. She'd seen patients, including her own mother, gasping for breath, even while on oxygen. Besides, Jane loved to look pretty, and how could she, if she had oxygen tubes in her nose? She loved to greet visitors at her church. How would people react to a woman with tubes in her nose? These anticipations filled her with despair.

Finally, after several years, Jane could no longer put off accepting oxygen. She prayed for peace about it and went for the tests and instruction. When the equipment arrived in her home, she had to live tethered to a twenty-five-foot tube which passed over her ears and into her nose. If she went out of the house, she had to fill her small tank and carry it, always taking care to keep it upright.

The day after the installation of all this equipment, Jane called me. I expected her to be in tears, but her voice was filled with joy. She said, "I asked God to help me, and I made up my mind I was going to accept this as a blessing. And it is! I have new energy. My oxygen tanks are actually my friends."

She gave her new friends names and put colorful stickers of smiley faces, butterflies, flowers, and funny sayings on "Lucy," her portable tank. Jane said, "I'm hoping if I cheerfully accept this equipment, so will other people. And it seems to be working."

Knowing Jane's intense aversion to wearing tubes in her nose, her peaceful acceptance seems like a touch from heaven. She has persuaded me that I too can find a bit of heavenly rest while here on earth. God can and will help us handle all the things that disturb our peace, but we can also help ourselves by changing our attitudes. Small, upward-bound attitudes will help us to "take heaven" now.

"Find rest, O my soul, in God alone; my hope comes from him. He alone is my rock and my salvation; he is my fortress, I will not be shaken" (Ps. 62:5-6).

O Lord our God, who gave us time and set us in it, you who rested from creation, show us what rest really is. When we pause to be quiet or pray, or when we lie down to sleep, fill us with your peace. You who know our deepest needs, touch us with heaven now. (EL)

Caring for Myself

As a teenager I was taught that it would someday be my responsibility to care for a family. At the age of sixteen my mother had had to quit school and take care of the home and family when her mother died. Like so many other females, I was taught that this was to be my responsibility as well. At no time was I taught to take care of myself.

As I struggled with a disabled spouse and six children, I discovered that my health was suffering. I had fallen into the trap of thinking that taking care of my own needs was selfish. I had not taken care of me, and I felt guilty whenever I wanted to.

Then I began to read more and more about Jesus as my example. I saw that he actually went off and rested. Jesus learned to balance his care of others with meeting his own physical and spiritual needs.

At first I couldn't see how I could possibly have a chance to take care of my own needs when I had no time alone. Then a daycare center opened for victims of Alzheimer's disease. It was a wonderful blessing to take Lee there and then go home and collapse for a couple of hours. I could read, write, or just plain sleep. I discovered that I was much easier to live with after those few hours alone. And on days when things would be a little bit rough at home, I'd remind myself that in a certain number of days, I'd have some time off.

You need time off as well. Find someone who can give you a break, and take it. Do not feel guilty. If Jesus needed time alone, we as caregivers certainly need time alone to be refreshed. I thank Jesus that he understands this.

"But Jesus often withdrew to lonely places and prayed" (Luke 5:16).

Father, I thank you for the rest you provide my body today. (MAM)

143

A Choice beyond Price

When a parent, spouse, adult child, or other family member becomes a caregiver, he or she knows it will cost something—time, energy, and emotional upheaval at the very least. Knowing a loved one is in need, the caregiver willingly chooses to pay the cost.

But the price tag of coming alongside and meeting the daily needs of another is always higher than any person can anticipate. The loss of personal freedom, the physical labor, the restructuring of everything in your life, the day and night responsibility—these things can make the price staggering at times.

I felt that way when caring for my emotionally troubled daughter. Often I didn't sleep. My stomach was tied in knots. And at times depression clung to me like a starfish to a pier piling. I prayed a thousand prayers for strength, for wisdom, for help. But finally I prayed, "The price is too high, Lord. I can't pay it."

God used my choice of terms to remind me of an Old Testament story about David. The details of it were sketchy in my mind, so I opened my Bible and found the story in 2 Samuel 24. A plague was killing the Israelites, but God had told David how to end it by offering a sacrifice at a specific location. The place turned out to be another man's barn, and he freely offered it to the king. But David responded that he wouldn't give something to God that cost him nothing.

Reading this event in the Bible did not change the price of caring for my daughter, but it did change how I looked at the price. I had been reminded that even as David wasn't forced to pay for his offering to God, I wasn't being forced to pay for mine. I had chosen to pay. I didn't have to be a caregiver. There were institutions that would take my daughter. I could even tell her to leave the house. But out of love for her and in obedience to what I felt God wanted me to do, I had chosen to provide the care she needed.

This reminder encouraged me. It took my load and turned it into a sweet-smelling sacrifice to God.

"No, I insist on paying you for it. I will not sacrifice to the Lord my God burnt offerings that cost me nothing" (2 Sam. 24:24).

Lord, thank you for reminding me that I am not a victim of caregiving. I have chosen to participate in it, and what it costs me only makes my sacrifice to you a sweeter one. (DH)

Ultimate Mercy

As caregivers, we often feel certain that if we look hard enough and pray long enough, we'll find a way to fix our problem. So the truth that we can't fix it, and God isn't going to fix it, often leaves us overwhelmed by the reality of our helplessness.

The day I faced my reality, I'd done all I could for my cancer-filled husband. I'd cleaned him. I'd made him comfortable. I'd given him his medicine. But still everything was the same. *There just has to be something else I can do,* I thought.

Prayer came to mind. But I'd prayed my heart out. What was left to pray for? I looked at my once-athletic husband's hollow cheeks and asked, *Where is your mercy, Lord?* Immediately I sensed an answer from God—"My mercy is not always the easy way."

The quick ease of God's answer pushed me out of the emotional stupor I was functioning in. I felt angry. I wanted to shake God. "You give me this trite answer when I'm watching the person I love most on earth die!"

God let me pour out the helplessness that made his mercy seem like such a trivial thing to me. Then, when my anger subsided, he brought another thought to my mind. "What if I weren't here?"

The question sucked the air out of me. Instantly I gasped, *Oh no, God.* Somehow in that brief second I realized that my husband would still be dying and I would still be helpless. Only there would be no one to talk to, cry with, seek strength from, or rage at. I would be alone—terribly alone.

Instead, I wasn't alone. God's mercy surrounded my husband and me. It wouldn't "fix it." It wouldn't take away my pain and loss. But his mercy would get me through in spite of my total helplessness. Later I read Lamentations 3:22-23 and underlined it. I knew it was true.

> *"Through the Lord's mercies we are not consumed, because his compassions fail not. They are new every morning; great is your faithfulness"* (Lam. 3:22-23, NKJV).

Lord, it is so easy to miss your mercy when I'm overwhelmed. Help me look for it in each of my days. (DH)

Not Forsaken

Some days when you've done all you can and prayed all you can, when nothing you do helps and it seems like God isn't helping, it's easy to feel forsaken. And yet, this is not true. To a Christian, forsaken is a feeling, not a fact.

When I can't understand God in the light of what's happening, I remember my friend Shirley, who was forsaken by every person she loved. She was in an auto accident that left her with minimal brain damage, changing her personality. When too many things came at her, she would panic and fly into a rage. After months of treatment and therapy, doctors told Shirley's husband she would never get any better. Her teenage daughter and son moved out, unable to cope with the changes in their mother. She was forsaken by old friends, and, finally, her husband left her.

The traumatic brain injury had robbed Shirley of many skills and abilities; now depression set in. While hospitalized, in spite of her own despair (or maybe because of it), Shirley noticed the pain on the faces of other brain-ill patients. She remembered her own faith in Christ and began to pray for each patient. Before long her days became taken up with prayer for others. The more she prayed for others, the more stable her own emotions grew. Soon she was released to live free again.

Each year since then, Shirley has improved, and now she is doing all the things the doctors said she would never be able to do. Her intercessory prayer for others actually helped to heal the damage to her cognitive skills as well as her depression.

After eleven years, Shirley could drive again. Today, nearly thirteen years after the accident, she continues to improve far beyond anything humanly possible. She speaks and teaches on the subject of intercessory prayer. She conducts several Bible clubs a week for neighborhood children. Most exciting, after years of not being trusted by her daughter, she gets to babysit her grandson. She has written and illustrated picture books for him, which a publisher is considering for publication.

Shirley says that although she felt forsaken, she knows now she never was. She still lives alone, not yet able to handle the routine of a regular job. Her disability pay ran out six years ago, but she prays about needs and has lacked nothing. To all who know her, Shirley is a living reminder that no matter how we may feel, we who believe in God are never forsaken.

We may have this hope for ourselves—that when we pray earnestly for others, somehow this gives God an open door to help us as well. Praying for others banishes the feeling of being forsaken and catapults us into vibrant fellowship with Christ.

> *"Anyone who is having troubles should pray. Anyone who is happy should sing praises. . . . When a believing person prays, great things happen"* (James 5:13,16, NCV).

O Lord our God, who made me for fellowship with others and with you, let me never be too busy to notice the needs of others and to pray for them as fervently as I pray for my own needs. Thank you for never forsaking me. (EL)

Never Forgotten

Whether it is a doctor's diagnosis or the whirling lights and piercing sirens of an ambulance, the initial trauma that brings the need for caregiving usually produces an outpouring of cards, flowers, gifts, and visits. Family and friends feel in some measure your shock, confusion, and emotional pain, and they try to encourage you.

As weeks and months pass, the shock wears off; the confusion becomes a day-by-day routine, and the emotional pain no longer produces a steady stream of tears. In addition, the flow of help from family and friends is reduced to a trickle. At these times it is so easy to feel alone—as if everyone's gone back to normal life but you.

I felt that way when my husband faced his third surgery. I knew most of the hospital nurses by name. I'd long ago adjusted to the medical smell. And I had a list of people who'd watch my four children. Art's cancer was now a part of our lives. So this time no flowers brightened his hospital room. Few cards filled our mailbox. And only a few family members stopped by.

That's when the letter from a distant friend arrived. It read, "I don't know exactly why I'm writing, but God brought you to my mind many times during this last week. I just wanted to let you know I was praying for you."

At first I was just grateful for my friend and her card. But later when I looked at the card again and reread it, I saw something that wiped away my discouragement. My friend didn't know about Art's illness. She didn't know he was having yet another surgery. But God did. He reached down to a friend living one thousand miles away from me and stirred her to pray for me. Though the short note wasn't the overt, obvious comfort of flowers and visits, it reminded me that God had not forgotten me.

I'd lost that truth when most of our friends' earlier attentiveness had ended. In the routine that followed, I had been blind to God's more quiet encouragement. But after my friend's letter, I began to look for it. I noted verses found on just the right days, timely phone calls, and times when things just went well. More and more I realized they were little gifts from God to assure me that he had not forgotten me.

> *"Can a woman forget her nursing child, and not have compassion on the son of her womb? Surely they may forget, yet I will not forget you. See, I have inscribed you on the palms of my hands"* (Isa. 49:15-16, NKJV).

Lord, it is so easy to let the demands of caregiving blind me to God's quiet encouragement. Help me to notice your great faithfulness every day. (DH)

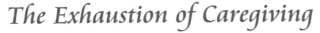

The Exhaustion of Caregiving

Tobey's wife, Irene, suffered from diabetes for most of her adult life. It was a continuous struggle to regulate her blood sugar. Tobey's most difficult time came when Irene's blood sugar was so low she would almost pass out. Tobey always had to be watchful, and quite often he became exhausted because of the constant care and concern.

He learned to tell when his wife needed some sugar, but Irene would often refuse to eat anything. As her blood sugar dropped, Irene would go to sleep. Tobey would shake her, trying to wake her up, but to no avail. If she did awaken some, she would shove Tobey away. The more she needed sugar, the more combative she would become. She refused to eat anything even though it meant saving her life. Tobey continued to struggle with this problem until her death.

While many women attend support groups or have a friend with whom they can share their concerns, most men do not. Tobey's only support came when he prayed and read his Bible. One time, as Tobey struggled not only with Irene but with his own exhaustion, he begged God to do something that would help him get some sugar into Irene. He was so frustrated and so exhausted he wanted to punch Irene to wake her up.

The Lord heard; Irene suddenly came to enough to realize she had to eat something, and she allowed Tobey to spoon some honey into her.

As long as we have God we are, like Tobey, not alone, but God often wants to use human hands to help us. This might mean bringing in someone to sit with the person you are caring for while you take a nap. It might also mean finding a support person. How wonderful to know that no matter what our personality, we can approach Christ in prayer with our concerns. He does understand, and he does care. We can rely on him.

> *"Be joyful always; pray continually; give thanks in all circumstances, for this is God's will for you in Christ Jesus"* (1 Thess. 5:16-18).

Father, thank you for helping each of us with our caregiving. Help me to remember, as I struggle with this situation, that you are here with me always. (MAM)

Never Alone

At my most exhausted times, at my most emotionally hurting moments as a caregiver, nothing seemed to help. Though I appreciated caring hugs and knew the value of prayer and Scripture, sometimes they just did not do anything. I was numb to the care of others, and my mind couldn't concentrate long enough to read God's words to me or even pour out my feelings to him.

At those points I could do little but simply cry to God for help. In every case the immediate effects of bottoming out did not go away. I still ached with hurt or felt tired beyond endurance. Sometimes as I wept or hung my head, God seemed to sit beside me, holding me in his arms. I still felt my pain and struggled to keep going, yet somehow, impossibly, I knew God's comfort.

At other times, I didn't even feel God's closeness. I remember once standing in the doorway of my husband's room, tired beyond words and holding on to the door frame. In total exhaustion, I told God, "You say you won't give me more than I can handle. Right now that doesn't feel true. I'm going to have to keep going on your promise alone. I have nothing else."

The rest of the night was long and hard, but I did make it. And like all of my seemingly blank answers from God, at some point after I could listen again and not just cry, something happened. At such times, God used Scripture, a thought, a song, or a conversation to show me he had been with me earlier when I felt myself hitting bottom.

All caregivers experience down times when nothing seems to help. God does not spare us from the pain and exhaustion of caregiving, but he never makes us go through it alone.

"Understand, therefore, that the Lord your God is the faithful God who for a thousand generations keeps his promises and constantly loves those who love him and who obey his commands" (Deut. 7:9, TLB).

When nothing helps . . . when you feel a million miles away . . . Lord, help me to still cling to you. (DH)

A Hand to Hold

Caregivers need care, especially for loneliness. I remember seeing the rest of the world go by with seemingly no problems, while I had to be strong for Mom, my grandchildren, and all the rest of my family. If my husband, Dick, felt well, I was okay, but if he was ill or depressed, I needed the comfort of knowing I wasn't totally alone. I needed a hand to hold.

Dick taught me the comfort and joy of having a hand to hold. On our first date, while we were walking in a park, a sudden summer rain soaked us. As we ran for the car, Dick grabbed my hand to help me keep up with his longer strides. My hand was so wet, it slipped from his grip. He tried to wipe it dry but only made it wetter. Laughing, he protectively tucked both of our hands inside his sport coat pocket. If I had not loved him already, I would have fallen for him at that moment.

Years later when I was in the hospital in labor, Dick sat beside me while we waited for the miracle of birth. At the onset of each contraction, Dick reached over and held my hand. Now that we are grandparents, I don't vividly remember the pain of that labor. As clearly as yesterday, however, I remember his strong, caring grip.

There have been times since then when I needed a hand to hold, and because of Dick's depression, he could not do it. The touch of God holding my hand has become as real as my husband's warm grip, even though at times I forget this is so until after a crisis has passed. God says, "For I am the Lord, your God, who takes hold of your right hand and says to you, 'Do not fear; I will help you'" (Isa. 41:13).

This truth does not cease to exist just because I can't see or feel God's hand on mine. When I was in labor, I didn't have to reach out for Dick's hand. He reached out for mine, refusing to leave me alone in my pain. Even more faithfully and tenderly, God, the source of all love, is there for me and will take care of me.

"You hold me by my right hand. . . . My flesh and my heart may fail, but God is the strength of my heart and my portion forever" (Ps. 73:23, 26).

Heavenly Father, hold my hand tightly when I feel alone in my pain and grief. Hold my hand just as I hold the hands of children, and walk with me. I know you will never let go of me or fail me. Thank you, Lord. (EL)

Mrs. Job

So often, as I've gone through the agony of watching my husband become just a shell of the man I married, I've felt all alone. When I searched the Scriptures for help, I turned to Mrs. Job. I have heard so many sermons on how she nagged her husband and asked him if he still held on to his integrity and suggested that he curse God and die.

I wish God had allowed us to see her later on. She too had lost everything, and now her husband was disabled. She was crushed, and, as I see it, she reacted in the only way she knew how. Nowhere does the Bible suggest that God punished her for this. I'm sure he understood her feelings of helplessness. I'm also sure that she and Job patched things up after he was healed, because they had more children to replace the ones killed.

While I did not lose my children when their father became disabled, I lost income as well as my husband's health. Until he went into a nursing home, I could not go out and earn money except through my writing. I was scared and somewhat afraid of the future. Mrs. Job was also afraid of the future.

I don't know why Mrs. Job told her husband to just die. Maybe she couldn't stand to see him suffer anymore and knew that death would relieve his suffering. Maybe she thought in her confusion that his death would make things better in life for her. I do know that since we all have the same feelings and emotions, many of us have reacted as Mrs. Job did. God understands, however, and forgives and continues to love and uphold us even in the darkest days.

Mrs. Job was fortunate. God eventually restored her husband to her. She was given a second chance to love and accept him and to raise another family with him. God has chosen not to heal my husband. He has assured me, though, that I am not all alone. I am part of a large group of spouses who care for a disabled partner, as well as many who care for other disabled family members. And God has promised me he is always with me.

Mrs. Job apparently did not have a support group she could join, but we have support groups available to us. Check your newspaper for lists of groups in your area, and also check with your church. If there is no support group for your particular caregiving situation, you can always start one. I was fortunate that someone told me about a support group almost as soon as I learned about Lee's disability. God uses people to remind me of his constant love and faithfulness even when I feel alone.

"Great is his faithfulness; his lovingkindness begins afresh each day" (Lam. 3:23, TLB).

Father, I thank you that you are always with me, every single day, when I'm in a supporting group and when I'm alone. (MAM)

Happiness Is Loving

Sometimes in caregiving, the one we care for is no longer able to communicate love. This is not only painful, but it is a uniquely lonely situation. Although we know they really would love us if they were themselves, over time we can begin to feel unloved.

If our loved one suffers from prolonged depression or another brain disability, how do we cope with a long-term loss of expressed love? I've found that losing love is not the same as being without love. We can't make others treat us lovingly, but being loved by our loved ones is only one side of the golden coin of love.

One time a young man told me, "I married my wife because I need her. This is all love is: needing someone." I argued, but not too loudly. Secretly I felt a grudging respect for his honesty. More than I wanted to admit, I'd been practicing what he preached—judging the quality of a loving relationship by how much I got out of it.

A song from a Broadway musical says the happiest people in the world are the ones who need people. This is partly true, but if we depend upon people to make us happy and to keep us feeling good about ourselves, we'll be exchanging the gold coin of love for a bag full of disappointment, betrayal, and loss.

When I fell in love with my husband, I made him my god. It took about three years for my hormone-induced insanity to subside. Finally, I could accept that he was only a normal, but good man. Nevertheless, the expectation that he should meet most of my needs had sunk roots deep in my soul. Years of living with his recurrent depressions, which did not always respond to medication, forced me to accept the obvious. The only safe place to go for my deepest needs was to the God who made me.

Poet Richard Crashaw, in an untitled poem he wrote in the seventeenth century, gave me an image of the love of Christ that never fails to unwind the shroud of my loneliness. He says,

> Nor can the cares of His whole crown
> (When one poor sigh sends for Him down)
> Detain Him, but He leaves behind
> The late wings of the lazy wind,
> Spurns the tame laws of time and place,
> And breaks through all ten heavens to our embrace.

I am so touched to think of Christ rushing faster than the wind to comfort me the instant I sigh. I choose to believe this is as true as the fact that God Is.

Once I am loved by God, I can loosen my grip on the gold coin of love, turn it over, and see the complete treasure. The other side contains a wondrous truth: we don't have to be loved by other people to live a life illumined by love. Jesus said it is more blessed to give than to receive. In the final say, giving love can bring more happiness than receiving love. And we can choose to love, for he commands us to love (John 15:12).

When the one you love cannot respond lovingly, ask God to fill you with so much of the passion of Jesus Christ that you may, by his nature, give from the well of God's love within you. Picture Jesus rushing to you faster than the wind.

While you still will miss the warm responses of your disabled loved one, God can ease the loneliness. It's a blessing to need the Lord Jesus and then to find him instantly with you. And it's an even greater blessing to pass on his unconditional love.

"If you obey my commands, you will remain in my love, just as I have obeyed my Father's commands and remain in his love" (John 15:10).

O God, our Father, I know you understand my loneliness and loss, because Jesus Christ suffered such awful loneliness in Gethsemane and during his trial. Please fill me to overflowing with your Spirit, the Companion your Son promised to send. Thank you for this great gift of love! (EL)

I Am Not Alone

Sometimes we feel that we are totally alone in facing the long years of caregiving. Diane is one person who has felt this way. Twelve years ago her husband had a cancerous brain tumor removed. He was left with the mind of a thirteen-year-old child. This slow march to the end of his illness has been the greatest trial of Diane's faith as she has tried to raise three children on her own.

Often during her earlier years of caregiving, Diane felt as if God had deserted her. However, she now believes God allowed this tragedy to happen for a reason. Even though the tumor is growing again in her husband's brain, Diane continues to believe that the cross they carry is going to result in good.

The story of Mary, Martha, and Lazarus has been a help to Diane. Like many of us, she has cried out to Christ, "If you had been here . . ."

Even though our own limited minds may see no purpose in all this suffering, someday we will know God as we are known by him. Then we will see his purpose. My prayer now for myself and for you is that by faith, instead of feeling unloved and forgotten by God, we will be able to praise him.

"I am the resurrection and the life. He who believes in me will live" (John 11:25).

Lord, help us to accept that you know the reason behind our suffering and that no matter the circumstances, you continue to love us. (MAM)

In Divine Company

When it comes to caregiving, the list of things that need to be done can seem overwhelming at times. Cooking special food, giving medications, helping with baths, cleaning messes, and getting up in the middle of the night—these tasks begin to define your life, and eventually someone calls you a "caregiver."

To be honest, I didn't really like the title. It somehow conjured up pictures of bedpans, pill bottles, and feeding spoons. I didn't mind being called a wife, a mother, a writer, a teacher, a daughter—but caregiver wasn't something I'd written down when my third grade teacher asked, "What do you want to be when you grow up?"

In spite of my attitude, there were some caregiving duties that I found comforting. One of those was helping my husband get dressed. The intimacy of the act, the tenderness of the moment somehow always took us back to the relationship we shared before he got sick. It was also through this act that God showed me what exceptional company I was in as a caregiver.

I was reading the familiar passage in Genesis that tells how Eve and Adam sinned and how God searched the Garden for them in the evening. When God found them, he disciplined them. Though this humanity-changing moment always causes me to pause, it was the next verse that made me see this familiar scene in a whole new way. It said that the Lord made garments and clothed Adam and Eve.

For the first time, I saw God as a caregiver. I knew the intimacy and tenderness of that moment of clothing another. I thought of my own gentleness in dressing arms made frail by illness. I remembered the incredible depth of unspoken words as I was entrusted with something that humbled yet helped my husband.

As a caregiver, it's so easy to feel as if God is a million miles away. Somehow his greatness doesn't seem to mix with soiled sheets and putting on socks. But long before we ever reached out our hands to give care, God reached out his.

"The Lord God made garments of skin for Adam and his wife and clothed them" (Gen. 3:21).

O Lord, when my tasks seem so lowly and mundane, help me remember that you, Creator of heaven and earth, did such things too. (DH)

A New Strength

The one thing every caregiver needs is strength. In the midst of special needs, night duties, and emotional drain, a person tending another is always on the edge of exhaustion. A good night's sleep is rare; a laid-back, relaxing day even rarer. Muscles ache. Attitudes droop. Sometimes you're so bodily tired, you feel disconnected, like you're outside yourself, watching as you trudge through what needs to be done.

Through it all, you keep praying, "Lord, please help me. Please give me strength." But no surges of stamina or lightning bolts of energy answer you.

More than once I questioned God's seeming lack of response. Why didn't he answer? Why didn't he help? Would he ever ease my weariness? I found my answer in a most unexpected place, and it made me rethink what God's strength truly looks like. While reading my Bible, I was with Jesus in the Garden of Gethsemane. He was praying into the night and absolutely weary with the anticipation of what lay before him. But then Luke 22:43 says that an angel came to strengthen him.

I don't know what I expected to follow this divine help—peace, renewed energy? But I didn't expect to read next the well-known verse about Jesus being in so much agony that his sweat became as drops of blood.

The order of events in these verses stopped me. After Jesus was strengthened, his agony continued, his prayers intensified, his sweat became as drops of blood. No surges of stamina. No lightning bolts of energy. As I realized what this meant, I asked God, "What is your strength, if not a feeling. When I pray for it, what does it bring?"

In answer, my thoughts traced through the events that followed Christ's prayer: his betrayal, arrest, trials, crucifixion, death, and resurrection. The divine strength given to Jesus did not miraculously whisk away his human exhaustion, pain, and suffering. The strength did, however, miraculously enable him to do what had to be done in a righteous way. He accomplished the will of his Father.

Though I want to do God's will even while caregiving, I must confess I often wish God's strength was a lightning bolt of energy. A few times it has been. But when it's not, I no longer feel as if my prayers for strength are unanswered. I know from Christ's example that, no matter how I feel after praying for strength, God is giving it.

> *"Then an angel appeared to him from heaven, strengthening him. And being in agony, he prayed more earnestly. [Then] his sweat became like great drops of blood falling down to the ground"* (Luke 22:43-44, NKJV).

Lord, I like lightning bolts and quick fixes. But help me treasure the divine strength that allows me to be totally human and yet still please God. (DH)

Choose Wisely

How can we lay down our lives for our disabled loved ones and still keep our own health and stability? Sometimes it's easy to feel we should join in the pain of our loved ones. Out of sympathy, we may mistakenly let their illness become our illness and we become disabled ourselves. Yet God did not give us the challenge of being disabled. God gave us the work of caring for the disabled. If we are to be strong enough to do his will, we must protect our emotional and physical health.

Sometimes the needs of our loved ones become a demanding god who dictates our every thought and action. However, our Creator designed us to have lives of our own, and then to freely give. He gave us a need for a certain amount of separateness from our loved ones.

Jesus showed us how to love greatly and keep a balance. Although he loved his mother, he didn't let Mary's worries dictate his actions. He loved Peter, but he didn't let Peter's fears keep him from laying down his life in Jerusalem. Throughout his ministry, he regularly withdrew from the crowds who needed him, even though he loved them enough to die for them.

Soren Kierkegard, a young Dane from the last century, gave me a fresh glimpse of this kind of balance. He said, "There is only one being whom a man may love better than himself: God. Therefore Christ does not say, 'Love God as yourself,' but 'Love God with all your heart, soul, and mind.'"

The Lord expects us to love ourselves as much as we love the ones we care for. While we care for them, we are to be our own caregivers too. When I am tempted to ignore my own needs, many of them God-ordained, I remember the holy order in Jesus' life. Each day I want to learn more about his way.

"Love the Lord your God with all your heart and with all your soul and with all your mind and with all your strength. . . . Love your neighbor as yourself" (Mark 12:30-31).

O Lord our God, please help me stay tender toward the one I care for and yet tough about taking care of myself. (EL)

Running on Empty

At times you probably feel as if you are running on an empty tank of gas. I remember one Tuesday evening when my daughters Sherri and Selena were arguing—not an unusual occurrence with teenage girls, but the results were unusual for most homes. Suddenly their father began to scream at Selena for something Sherri had just said. He was having a catastrophic reaction to a simple problem, typical to Alzheimer's patients. When I stepped in to calm everyone down, Lee grabbed my hand and in his frustration bent one of my fingers backwards, tearing a ligament.

The next Sunday, two of the kids had an argument in the van on the way to church. We settled everything, but at lunch time, Lee reacted as if the argument had just happened and began to yell at the two children involved. It took several minutes to calm him down. Then my youngest came to me in tears because he had tried to hug his dad and had been pushed away.

I collapsed on the chair and cried. I had no energy left to deal with any more of the catastrophic reactions this brain disease caused in our family. My "gas tank" was on empty.

"God, where are you?" I cried out. "You just don't understand all that I'm going through."

As I sobbed, I began to see a picture in my mind. Jesus Christ stood there holding out his hands. The nail scars appeared red and sore. Then I saw him standing in front of the tomb of his friend Lazarus. He had lost a friend, and he hurt. Other images came into my mind—Jesus being misunderstood by his brothers and sisters and being spat on just before he was crucified, his disciples denying and betraying him.

What did Jesus do when his "gas tank" became empty? I knew that was when he went off to talk with his heavenly Father. God didn't change any of the circumstances Jesus had to face here on earth, but he did give his Son the strength to go through each one.

I took my Bible out onto our deck and sat on the porch swing and read and prayed. I knew the circumstances weren't going to change overnight, but the Lord refilled my gas tank, and I was ready to face the next set of catastrophic reactions.

Maybe it's not easy to get off by yourself as Jesus did. I know there were times when the only place I could be alone was in the bathroom. I not only brought my Bible or another book into the bathroom; I often brought my writing.

It seems that Jesus' main concern when he was running on empty was to get away from people and be alone with God until he felt renewed. A few minutes alone with God will fill our gas tanks too.

"For we do not have a high priest who cannot sympathize with our weaknesses, but was in all points tempted as we are, yet without sin" (Heb. 4:15, NKJV).

Dear Lord, Thank you for being there for me and refilling my gas tank. (MAM)

Lightening the Load

Emotions and work. All too often these two grind against each other in the caregiver's life. Too many tears. Not enough sleep. Too many mind-churning fears. Not enough energy.

This draining duo can only go on for so long. As we grapple to cope, the physical work doesn't go away, so eventually we restrain our emotions. Consciously or unconsciously we say, "I can't deal with this anymore, Lord," and somewhere inside of us we flip our emotion switch to "off."

I faced this as a single parent caregiver, trying to deal with a daughter making poor choices. I tried to keep functioning, but every phone call, every slammed car door, every squeaking floor board triggered a rush of pain and indecision. I stayed agitated by day and sleepless by night.

Though I often called family or friends seeking answers, it didn't help. Their suggestions always lacked a vital element—they didn't have to live with the end results. So I see-sawed between indecision and reacting out of pain. It had to stop.

Finally one evening I curled up in my overstuffed recliner. Weeping, I told God, "I love Janet so much, but I can't deal with her. The love I have for her as a mom gets muddled up with what I must do. I've got to set aside my feelings. But I'm afraid I'll stop loving her and get hard."

Putting my hands together and holding them open toward heaven, I pictured them holding my innermost feelings for my daughter. Then I said to God, "Lord, will you take my feelings? Will you guard them until I can safely have them back again?"

Though I continued to cry, the double load I'd been carrying felt lightened. In the days that followed I somehow started sleeping more. And somehow I began to act.

During those days, I made some of the hardest decisions of my life. After I made each one, a rush of breath-sucking hurt would engulf me, and I'd cry. I dreaded those hurt-and-cry times until one day I realized God was answering my prayer. I was functioning and deciding, but I was also feeling. Only now the two things weren't all muddled together. Somehow God had placed them side-by-side in my life.

"You have seen me tossing and turning through the night. You have collected all my tears and preserved them in your bottle! You have recorded every one in your book. The very day I call for help, the tide of battle turns. My enemies flee! This one thing I know: God is for me!" (Ps. 56:8-9 TLB).

My emotions and workload are too heavy, Lord. I want to do the work and shut off my feelings. But somehow help me deal with both. (DH)

At the End of the Rope

When I was a child, a movie came out called *Each Dawn We Die.* I don't know what it was about, but I've never forgotten that gripping title. As a caregiver, sometimes I felt that each day was a small death for myself and for my mom.

During a bleak time I wrote in my journal, "I promised myself that I would keep enough joy in my life that I would never find myself wishing Mom would die and get it over with. But I have failed." For many caregivers the only physical relief will be when their loved one dies. We don't want that to happen, but our doubts and thoughts are real.

While we may want the suffering of our loved one to end, none of us wants our own wishes to involve the end of life for someone else. In my case, I reached the end of my rope after I had started going twice a week, for a day and a night, to stay with my mom who lived fifty miles away. I was also working thirty hours a week in a dental office and learning to write for publication. My son had recently moved home after his wife walked out and I had become a surrogate mother for my two grandchildren, ages eighteen months and three years. I was stretched too far physically. No longer did I have time or energy for anything but responsibilities—no more hiking, bicycling, painting, or reading a good book.

After pouring out my feelings of despair in my journal, I turned my mind to the Lord, or, more accurately, he turned my mind to him. Then I wrote, "We all die many deaths before we get to that last open door. In Christ we die daily, giving up things we want for the needs of others. In living for Christ, only through death does new life come. There is no Easter without Good Friday first."

174

Christ brings forth life from every relinquishment we make in his name. So when the cocoon of caregiving draws closer and closer, we can spiritually rest in the cocoon, letting him make of us what he desires.

For me, resting in the cocoon meant planning better. In order to have quiet time, I woke up two hours before anyone needed me, which meant going to bed as early as I could. Whenever possible, I piggy-backed one activity on another, doing sit-ups while in the bathtub and muscle-tension exercises while driving.

As I took care of myself spiritually and physically, my mental and emotional balance returned. I "died" to many activities I'd enjoyed, but I was more alive for Mom and my grandchildren and my husband and son.

If we are living for Christ, each dawn we'll die a little to ourselves. When we do, a day of joy will come, for we'll be more like him! The cocoon that was our death will be like all empty cocoons, useless now that we have grown wings and our season in life has changed. Best of all, our loved one will have been loved with the love of Christ.

"I can do everything through him who gives me strength" (Phil. 4:13).

O Lord our God, you made me and know my weakness. Grant me strength to keep on in quiet trust. Where I am weak, strengthen. When I need rest, help me to relax and rest in you. (EL)

God's Hiding Place

Years ago I became aware that I needed to set aside a place and a few moments of solitude each day. A secret spot, a hiding place, allowed me to be completely transparent and honest before the Lord.

When I was the young mother of two boys, ages one and four, we rented a house that threatened to tumble down if one of us sneezed extra hard! But it boasted the redeeming feature of a lovely old weeping willow tree out back. When my little ones napped, I parted the supple branches of that tree, that secret spot, and poured out an overflowing heart to my God. I was so new to this mothering thing (just as now I am new to caregiving) and felt so inadequate.

I'll admit that in those years I didn't listen to the Lord much, but now I understand the value of a two-way conversation—the importance of prayerfully asking what he wants to do in my topsy-turvy life, then listening for an answer. Sometimes it comes from his Word: "You are my hiding place; you will protect me from trouble and surround me with songs of deliverance" (Ps. 32:7).

I thank God for providing that sheltering, weeping willow back in the 1950s, just as I thank him today for providing himself as my minute-by-minute hiding place. In his presence, the pressure relaxes, and I can function again. I have fresh hope.

There are times when it is difficult to believe in the future because we have some of the Cowardly Lion in us. These are the times when we must concentrate on the present, must find that present note of joy, until courage returns. Perhaps it will be the robin tugging on a worm outside, or the telephone call of a friend, or the book you can hardly wait to finish reading.

Appreciate the present until strength comes to think about tomorrow.

> *"For in the time of trouble he shall hide me in his pavilion; in the secret place of his tabernacle he shall hide me; he shall set me high upon a rock"* (Ps. 27:5, NKJV).

"O Lord, the house of my soul is narrow; enlarge it, that you may enter in." These words of Saint Augustine echo so beautifully my own shrunken condition on some caregiving days. Please stretch my horizons and my concept of your magnitude, God. (LDV)

Take Rest

How can we rest when the needs of the one we love are unending? I remember how sorry I felt for my mother when she was caring for Dad. While we all helped some, she had his care at night, waking to get him a drink or to fetch the urinal, or just being kept awake because, childlike, he wanted to talk.

Then a few years later, I was staying with Mom and praying she would sleep through the night.

One evening after I had tucked her in bed, I was not only tired, but so tense I ached. On the way to Mom's house I had narrowly missed colliding with another car on the freeway, just because I was so tired I'd become inattentive. I lay down on my foam pad bed in the living room, desperate for sleep before Mom would call me in a couple of hours. My whole body felt like a violin string tuned too tight.

As I prayed for God to help me relax, my eyes fell on the silhouette of Mom's old oak rocking chair. I remembered how, when I was eight years old with the measles, she had come to my bed after preparing supper for our large family. She'd said, "You're a big girl now, but not too big to be rocked." Wrapping me in a cozy hand-made quilt, she carried me to the rocking chair in the living room and rocked me for endless wonderful minutes.

Now, looking at the rocking chair standing almost in the same place in the small living room, I remembered the comfort, peace, and security I'd felt in her arms. In her arms all my aches had melted away. I mused that if I could be rocked in her arms again, I could rest, but now she needed me to rock her. Suddenly on impulse I prayed, *Heavenly Father, would you hold me on your lap and rock me like my mother did?*

I didn't get up and go to the chair. I simply imagined that my pillow was my heavenly Father's shoulder and the foam pad under me was his lap. After a few quiet breaths, peace stole over me. I relaxed and rested in comfort as real as my memory of Mom's arms around me. In a few minutes I was sound asleep.

Since then, when I can't sleep, I often imagine I'm on God's lap. This never fails to relax and comfort me. God loves and cradles us in many ways we do not know and cannot perceive. His Spirit can meet us through our imagination and whisper peace to our spirits.

"Come to me, all you who are weary and burdened, and I will give you rest. Take my yoke upon you and learn from me, for I am gentle and humble in heart, and you will find rest for your souls" (Matt. 11:28-29).

Dear Lord, I come to you as your child. Hold me in your arms and help me to feel the comfort of being held. Let me relax against you physically as well as spiritually. Rest me and renew me as only you can. Thank you! (EL)

The Potter and the Clay

Have you ever watched a potter at work? My daughter took a pottery class and learned about forming bowls and other items. She learned that it takes a lot of hard work to make something perfect. Many times the clay has to be pounded down and put back into a ball because the potter needs to start the item over again.

In Jeremiah, we read that God is the potter and we are the clay. Can you imagine the clay deciding to jump off the wheel and run away because it didn't like the way it was being designed? Recently when I had one of those days when I wanted to run away, I was reminded of the potter and the clay. The potter can make a beautiful vase, or he can make a pot that will carry drinking water. The vase is a showpiece; the water pot has a purpose.

We are all God's treasures, and he is making us for his special purposes. Even as a caregiver, I'm being molded by God into the type of person he wants me to be. He has a purpose for my life.

On days when you want to jump off the Potter's wheel, try to imagine you are a lump of clay, still pliable, and that God is lovingly making you into the object he desires.

> *"But we have this treasure in jars of clay to show that this all-surpassing power is from God and not from us"* (2 Cor. 4:7).

Father, thank you for reminding me that you are making me into the object of your desire. Forgive me when I want to jump off the wheel. (MAM)

What If . . .

For as long as I can remember, I've given a lot of energy to shouldering an emotional backpack full of "what-ifs." I'm the one who takes a quart of drinking water on a half-hour bicycle ride. I carry three sets of car keys fastened to my body at any given time, even when I ride in someone else's car. In the middle of summer, just in case, my quilted parka goes into my car with me for the trip to the grocery store. I make lists of long-term and short-term goals and check off my progress at day's end with godly sorrow and trepidation. If I don't keep a written record, how will I know what to do tomorrow?

At age six, before I had heard the Boy Scouts' motto, "Be prepared," I began to practice it and protected myself from a few hurts during my school days. Therefore, in the adult world, I put serious effort into being prepared for anything. And then our second baby died; and my thirty-three-year-old sister died; and my husband's depressions took away his companionship. Soon stress gave me various miserable illnesses. It didn't take a lot of thinking to see that I needed to count on God, not me.

John Newton said,

> We judge of things by their present appearance, but the Lord sees them in their consequences; if we could do so likewise, we should be perfectly of his mind; but as we cannot, it is an unspeakable mercy that he will manage for us, whether we are pleased with his management or not.

It's not easy for a habitual "scout" to let tomorrow be God's business, but I'm trying. I pray that you, also, will remember that he wants to carry all your "what-ifs."

> *"Which of you by worrying can add a single minute to (your) life? . . . as your first duty keep on looking for his standard of doing right, and for his will. So never worry about tomorrow"* (Matt. 6:27, 33-34, WILLIAMS).

Most loving God, it is such a mercy to know that you manage my tomorrows. Thank you! And thank you for helping me not to confuse the wisdom of being prepared with the foolishness of trying to prevent every possible problem. (EL)

Abigail

When you were faced with the position of caregiver, you probably searched for answers. In the early days after Lee was diagnosed with Alzheimer's disease, I searched the Bible to find any women who had to cope with a disabled husband. I wanted to know how they reacted to losing their husband.

One woman I found was Abigail. Her husband, possibly an alcoholic, had a different problem than Lee, but I did learn from her situation. I read and re-read her story, trying to imagine what life was like for her before 1 Samuel 25. Why did Nabal become an alcoholic? How did this affect their marriage? What could I learn from this? Since Lee's behavior often resembled what I had heard happened to an alcoholic, I wanted to know what she did that I could do.

The most important thing I learned was that Abigail did not try to change her husband. She knew what he was. Her early dreams of what marriage would be like were probably shattered as mine had been. Abigail had no idea that one day she would be the wife of a king, but she accepted her husband for what he was and in the condition he was.

Abigail's acceptance did not change her husband's condition, but I'm sure it changed her. She didn't give in to self-pity, and I decided that I would not give in either. When I was tempted to do so, I would remember that I had children to raise and a house to run. It was important that I do it right and not moan and groan. I learned to accept Lee for what he was. I learned to enjoy the good days and to remember that the bad days were due to his illness, not his choice.

Abigail was not afraid to step in and take on her husband's responsibility when Nabal showed himself incapable. When it was necessary, I also learned to step in and do what had to be done without trying to explain to Lee what I was doing. Any explanation only caused a catastrophic reaction.

As God gave Abigail the strength to handle her husband, so he will also give you and me the strength to deal with our situation. Not one year at a time, but one day at a time.

"You therefore must endure hardship as a good soldier of Jesus Christ" (2 Tim. 2:3, *NKJV*).

Lord, help me to live just today. Please take care of my tomorrows as you have taken care of my yesterdays. (MAM)

Take Trust

When we've had to accept painful circumstances, such as the illness or disability of our loved one, the fearsome facts of today can turn into mountains of dread about what tomorrow will bring.

After working all day, when Mom called me for the third or fourth time during a night, I often had a hard time getting back to sleep. Then worry would come creeping into bed with me. How would we get along while one of my sisters, my fellow caregiver, had surgery? How would I finish that complicated dental bridge, back home in the office, by the time the patient arrived to have it placed? After gnawing on that problem for a while, I'd worry about whether I'd have to drive home in the snow. The fact that I couldn't *do* anything about these future problems did not deter me from working on them in my mind, instead of resting and sleeping.

Fortunately I learned that one way we can chase away the haunting future is to count our blessings, even in the middle of the night. As Cardinal John Henry Newman said in *Parochial and Plain Sermons:* "Let us try to gain a truer view of what we are, and where we are, in his kingdom. Let us humbly and reverently attempt to trace his guiding hand in the years we have hitherto lived."

When I count my blessings, I begin with the time I had a benign, but life threatening, uterine tumor. I hemorrhaged dangerously on the way to the hospital and was revived with a blood transfusion. Six weeks later, the doctor told me that the tumor could return if he had missed a single cell during his surgery. If it did, it would be highly malignant, and, connected directly to my bloodstream as a placenta would be, it would move swiftly throughout my body. For the next three years I must undergo frequent tests.

More than anything in the world, I feared cancer. In a state of near panic, I drove home praying, *Lord, you know me! You know I can't live with fear for three years!*

Quiet thoughts dropped into my mind. *You could have died if that tumor had grown much larger. Even as it was, you could have bled to death on the way to the hospital. Would I preserve your life through that to let you die of cancer?*

No, Lord, you wouldn't do that! I'd never been so sure of anything in my life. I was utterly at peace, confident that I didn't have to worry about cancer.

The tumor never returned, and through the three years of testing I never had a fear. Now, whenever I remember that solid, almost three-dimensional, inner assurance, my faith still leaps up to give me peace.

As we add up the good things God has done for us, our faith will grow strong enough to move mountains of worry. Remembering past blessings today blesses us all over again.

"You who live in the shelter of the Most High, who abide in the shadow of the Almighty, will say to the LORD, 'My refuge and my fortress; my God, in whom I trust'" (Ps. 91:1-2, NRSV).

Our Father, please forgive us for worrying, and help us to turn away from the temptation to borrow tomorrow's troubles for today. Refresh our memories of your blessings, and tuck us in safely, under your wing. (EL)

Only Today

More than any other time in my life, when I was a caregiver, I struggled under a burden of dread about what might happen. I wept so much for Mom and the suffering I anticipated for her, that I didn't fully enjoy her in the present moment.

Recently I learned better how to make the most of the present moment, because, in truth, right now is really all we have. I'm embarrassed to say I learned this from caring for my dog!

Jock is a lovable Welsh Corgi, a posthumous gift from my mother. Before Mom died, she said she wanted us to use the bit of money she would leave for something we especially wanted. I wanted a special companion dog. After research into the inherent qualities of a number of breeds, I decided on a Corgi. Jock turned out to be all I had wished for, and he reminded me daily of my mother's love for me.

When Jock was twelve, he developed a spinal nerve disease. Surgery had not helped. His hind legs grew spastic. The sight of him, unable to walk without support, broke my heart. As his disability worsened, I realized we might have to have him put down. Every time I looked at him, I wanted to cry. I couldn't bear to think of taking him to the vet that last time. I felt chronically grieved, just as I had when my mother was failing. I prayed for Jock to get better, just as I'd prayed for her.

And then one day, I looked at him and realized that he still was not in pain, and that I didn't know if I would ever have to have him put to sleep. I was agonizing over what might happen, and my attitude kept me from enjoying him for as long as he could stay and be my buddy. Suddenly I thought, *I did this with Mom, too. I made her a symbol of pain and loss, instead of just loving her at the moment.*

Jock had always delighted me, and just to look at him made me smile. I thought about how he was a gift from Mom. She would want me to receive joy, not sadness from him—even now at the end of his life. So I set my mind to keep on enjoying Jock and letting him know he's appreciated. It worked. It moved intense grief out and thanksgiving in. Now I thank God for each day Jock remains free of pain and can keep me company while I write.

Obviously, this attitude is easier to achieve with a pet than with a beloved person. But it is possible—and even necessary—to focus on right now and somehow make the cares of tomorrow become untouchables. God is ahead of us preparing our way for tomorrow as well as watching over us now. Shall we play God and try to live in tomorrow right along with today? Or can we trust the next hour to the one who loves us more than we can love him?

"When my spirit grows faint within me, it is you who know my way" (Ps. 142:3).

Heavenly Father, forgive us for not keeping our minds and hearts on this present moment where you have placed us. Grant us, please, more faith to let go of worries about the future and to live and love fully right now. (EL)

What about Today?

Often caregiving produces tender moments and deeper relationship, but sometimes the thought of it lasting for any length of time can produce feelings of fear or dread. Sharing such feelings inevitably brings the comment, "You just have to take it one day at a time."

There is a tremendous amount of truth in this statement, but it doesn't always encourage. It doesn't move the caregiver past thoughts such as *Lord, I can't take this for much longer.* Or, *I just can't go on like this for month after month.*

God must have known the "one day at a time" phrase would become an irritating cliché to me because, whenever I looked at my future and cried out, "I can't do this!" he never brought it to mind. Instead, he made the same truth real to me in a different way.

As a thirty-four-year-old caregiver, nursing my sick husband and raising our four children, many times I'd think about the weeks, months, or years ahead and end up crying. Each time I brought my tears to God, he'd whisper in my thoughts, *What about today? Have I given you enough grace to make it?*

Inevitability I responded, *Yes, Lord, but I can't keep this up. I can't keep going.*

But what about right now, today? Are you OK? Do you need more of anything?

At every question I had to admit that, for the moment, I was OK.

No matter how many times I tried to reach ahead with my anxiety, God never said, "Don't do that." Instead his concerned question continually

190

brought my focus back to the here and now. In the end, I'd finally quiet my pleas, and my heart would get the point—my present needs were met.

Just as he gave manna to the Israelites daily in the wilderness, God always provided for the day.

For every caregiver, there are times when seemingly endless tomorrows weigh heavy. At those moments, listen for God's voice. He is the only one who can say, "But what about today?" without it sounding like a cliché.

"Morning by morning they gathered it, as much as each needed; but when the sun grew hot, it melted" (Exod. 16:21, NRSV).

Lord, it is easier to say "Live one day at a time" than to do it, especially for the caregiver. Only you can make that eternal truth fresh and new for each of us today. (DH)

Seeing the Truth

When we are helping a permanently disabled loved one, the future can look dark and foreboding. At times all we can see is what can possibly go wrong or, in some cases, increasingly difficult times we are certain to face.

When we can't see the future, we form a distorted opinion of it in our imaginations. In an old book, I read about a painting called "Cloudland." The painter's name was not given, but the subject intrigued me. "Cloudland" hung in a German art gallery before World War II. From a distance it looked like an ugly, rolling mass of storm clouds, hideous and terrifying, painted in a dark confusion of colors.

If you were in that gallery and walked closer, however, the senseless daubs of paint would begin to take on form and shape. From a closer position you would see the truth—that the clouds were really masses of exquisite little angels and cherubim. In place of the sense of threat, you would find beauty and comfort.

Although showing an imaginary scene, the painting communicates a piercing truth. Things usually look more intimidating beforehand than when we get there. Furthermore, God does have angels all around us and angels waiting for us in the future, too. From the distance time creates, we may see our days as filled with heavy, dark clouds, but when we get there, we shall know God's comfort and help.

For our God is a God who comforts. He says through Isaiah:

"Shout for joy, O heavens;
Rejoice, O earth;
Burst into song, O mountains!

For the LORD comforts his people
and will have compassion on his afflicted ones"
(Isa. 49:13).

This is the truth. If we let dread of the future oppress us, we will miss his comfort today. In faith we can know that each moment, as the future becomes now, God is blessing us. Let's look with the eyes of our heart for God's gifts of love today. Our cloudlands right now are full of unseen angels.

"As it is written: 'No eye has seen, no ear has heard, no mind has conceived what God has prepared for those who love him'—but God has revealed it to us by his Spirit" (1 Cor. 2:9-10).

Lord, my way is painful, and sometimes I wonder where you are. Today, I need to know your love. Help me to see your gifts to me today, whether in a blossom, a bird, a snowflake, the caring words of a friend, or the words of the Bible. And when I am too tired to read your words in these many forms, touch my dreams and my sleep with your peace. (EL)

Rediscovering Joy

Battles with physical fatigue and emotional stress are common to caregivers. It is also obvious that these aren't easy struggles to overcome. Yet in and of themselves these are secondary issues. Though it is hard, we can live with feeling tired. And though we wish them away, we can deal with times of fear or worry. More significant, something that can make the thought of another day seem absolutely unbearable, is a lack of joy.

Joy is not just our smiles and laughter, but an inner spark that keeps us grabbing hold of every bit of goodness. It eventually sees God at work in even the hardest days. It clings to eternal hope even when the realities of earth seem bigger than all else. It's what motivates us to care for the needs of others, just as it motivated Jesus to endure the cross.

Perhaps one of the most discouraging or scariest experiences for caregivers is to realize they've lost their joy. They still go through the motions, but it's as if someone blew out their inner spark. I felt that way when year after year I single-parented a rebellious teen. I lost sight of the goodness of my other three children. I went to church but felt dry as a desert. I dealt with problems but never thought they would eventually end. I could remember previous joy, but I could not experience it.

I'd been praying about missing joy for some time, but my blown-out spark had a way of making prayer even feel useless. That's when God had a pastor quote a verse. This pastor actually spoke for almost forty minutes, but it was the verse that caught my attention and helped me rediscover my joy: "The prospect of the righteous is joy" (Prov. 10:28).

These seven words somehow turned me around. They started watering my desert, opening my eyes to my godly children, and making me believe that even my worst troubles would someday end.

> *"Looking unto Jesus, the author and finisher of our faith, who for the joy that was set before him endured the cross, despising the shame, and has sat down at the right hand of the throne of God"* (Heb. 12:2, NKJV).

Lord, we can't go to a store or even to a church to get some joy. Joy depends on you alone. For caregivers asking to rekindle their inner spark, please give each one a special, personal joy verse. (DH)

Hope That Holds On

Sometimes we caregivers plod through weeks and months when our nerves go on a rampage, when we feel pulled through the proverbial knothole. And because that knothole usually is too small or too irregular in shape, it hurts. We hope in God, however, because we know he is faithful in all his promises to us.

It is easier to hold onto genuine hope when I realize that God has never failed and therefore will not fail me now. His promises can spark warmth in my sometimes chilly and numb heart.

It seems to me that quite a difference exists between being hopeful—hoping for a sunny day this weekend or hoping that the doctor will return your telephone call soon—and a life that is filled with hope. Many people apply a different meaning to the word hope than God does in his Word: "We have this hope as an anchor for the soul, firm and secure" (Heb. 6:19).

Thumbing through a magazine at my dentist's office, I found a thought-provoking analogy that added a sparkle to the wobbly hope I possessed that afternoon. Elisabeth Kübler-Ross proposed that "people are like stained glass windows; they sparkle and shine when the sun is out, but when the darkness sets in, their true beauty is revealed only if there is a light from within."

I need to put myself where God can shine through, so I can be a lighted window for my loved ones, and a source of hope.

"Though the fig tree does not bud and there are no grapes on the vines, though the olive crop fails and the fields produce no food, though there are no sheep in the pen

and no cattle in the stalls, yet I will rejoice in the Lord, I will be joyful in God my Savior" (Hab. 3:17-18).

Heavenly Father, may I have more of that light from within that makes hope a tangible thing. A Chinese proverb says that a bird does not sing because it has an answer; it sings because it has a song. Even though I don't have many answers, give me your song of hope, Lord. (LDV)

Memories

In some illnesses, for caregivers, memories of the good times can be destroyed by the pain of the present. What can we do when we can't remember the good times? God does have some answers.

After Lee went into a nursing home, I realized that Alzheimer's disease had not only robbed my husband of his memories, it had also robbed me of the good memories of our marriage. All I could remember were Lee's moments and days of anger, frustration, and violence during the couple of years before the diagnosis, as well as the many years after. I cried out to God for his mercy.

I read in Jeremiah 31:15-16:

"A voice is heard in Ramah, mourning and great weeping, Rachel weeping for her children and refusing to be comforted, because her children are no more." This is what the Lord says: "Restrain your voice from weeping and your eyes from tears, for your work will be rewarded."

Verse 17 adds, "'There is hope for your future,' declares the Lord."

There was hope for my future, even in the midst of my weeping. I decided I needed to deliberately remember the good times we'd shared. After prayer, a couple of the things I did were to listen to the cassette tape of our wedding and look through our family photo albums.

I found I could do some things with other people that Lee and I had enjoyed, such as look for bells that we began collecting on our honeymoon or go to summer concerts in the park. Sometimes memories came at the price of tears. As a friend and I watched TV together, I remembered, for the first time in years, how Lee and I used to snuggle on the couch after the kids were in bed. After the initial pain of remembering, it became a good memory.

Lee used to love to cook Mexican food. After he was no longer capable of cooking, I just couldn't make the hot sauce he'd made from scratch. I always had excuses whenever the kids asked me to make it. When I finally decided I needed to do it for me, I called my friends John and Marion and invited them over for a Mexican dinner. I not only cooked the full meal; I made the hot sauce from scratch. Tears flowed as I made the sauce, but now I can fix that recipe without adding tears to it.

Although the memories of the last fifteen years are often difficult, the Lord has helped me to remember the first few years, which were full of laughter, love, adventure, and caring.

I believe that what we really need to know is the dimension of God's love. We need to know that no matter what the circumstances, we can depend on his love for us. Ask the Lord to use the memories of the past to encourage you now, and let the Holy Spirit comfort you.

> *"Therefore you now have sorrow; but . . . your heart will rejoice, and your joy no one will take from you" (John 16:22, NKJV).*

Some day, Lord, when you take my loved one home, I know his memories will be restored for him as well. That will truly be a day to rejoice. (MAM)

When God Doesn't Heal Now

Some truths are very painful to bear, and this is one: some of us and some of our loved ones won't be healed totally until we get to heaven. And we won't know why.

If our loved ones are not healed, they, and we, still live in the center of God's love—as much so as those whose loved ones are miraculously healed. Because we belong to Christ, we can know that suffering, when placed in God's loving hands, will never be in vain.

When my sister Lois suffered a debilitating, incurable illness for seven years and died at age thirty-three, it broke my heart. However, the day before she died, her heart stopped, and she had a near-death experience. She said she saw heaven and talked with God. For her last twenty-four hours on earth, she told her husband and our mother about the beauty and wonder and love of God.

Her experience greatly comforted Mom. Lois had died of pneumonia because her chronic disease prevented her from clearing her lungs. Before her heart stopped, she'd been on oxygen. After they revived her, she never felt a need for oxygen. During her final hours, she was comfortable and filled with joy. Knowing this, I was comforted.

When my sister's daughter, Judy, grew up, I learned that no one had told her about her mother's near-death experience. So I sent a written description of how her mother had talked with God. The story about Lois's last hours comforted Judy and strengthened her faith. Now she carries the story in her Bible and tells others, when someone needs comfort.

I also tell others who need comfort. Sometimes I try to imagine how far this story of the love of God may go to strengthen people who are in the midst of painful unanswerable questions. I cannot know, but I know it can bring a heavenly touch, and the circle of comfort will grow, because God is like that. He brings good out of everything that happens to those who love him.

Every one of us must die, one way or another, but no one who loves God dies in vain. God, who counts the hairs on our heads, cares about suffering and death. If he doesn't heal our loved ones for longer life here, he heals them perfectly by taking them to heaven. The one thing that Lois said over and over again after she returned from near death was this: "God told me I would be completely healed!" And she was.

Part of the Jewish Kaddish, the beautiful mourner's prayer, says, "The Lord shall be your everlasting light and the days of your mourning shall be ended. He will utterly destroy death forever; and the Lord God will wipe the tears from every face." This age-old promise to the Jews is repeated for us in the New Testament Revelation of the apostle John.

> *"God himself will be with them. . . . He will wipe every tear from their eyes. There will be no more death or mourning or crying or pain, for the old order of things has passed away" (Rev. 21:3-4).*

O God our Father, comfort me through the hard times of seeing my loved one suffer. Help me to remember the suffering of your Son and the truth that you chose to enter human flesh and share my pain. Please grant me patience and fill me with faith that grows stronger each day. (EL)

God's Plan for Me

I can see some of God's plan for me in several areas of my life that have become stronger because of the circumstances God has allowed to come to me.

Shortly after I accepted Christ when I was eleven years old, I read *Little Women*. I didn't know it then, but the Lord was planting seeds in my heart. I wanted to be just like Jo March. I wanted a house full of kids, and I wanted to write. For years I thought that my dreams must not have been God's dreams because none of them took place. I had one child, and, since my first husband left me when my son was a baby, I thought I would never have any more. As far as my writing went, I sent a short story to a magazine when I was seventeen, and when it was rejected, I thought that meant I couldn't write.

Then, when my son was twelve years old, God sent Lee, a widower with three children, into my life. Before my husband's illness we adopted two more children and had nine exchange students. The Lord also used Lee to encourage me to write. Starting when Lee went on disability, a lot of what I have written has been about what God has taught me through Lee's illness.

Through Habakkuk 2:2-3 God told me, "Write the words that I will give you." When I obey my Lord and write what he has given me, not only are others blessed, but I am blessed.

Ask God what his plans are for you. Sometimes he uses the rough times to help us fulfill these plans. No matter what our circumstances are, God can and will use them to honor and glorify himself and also to ultimately bless us. I'm so glad he does.

"Commit to the Lord whatever you do, and your plans will succeed" (Prov. 16:3).

Heavenly Father, help me to keep my eyes on you so I can share what you want shared with others. (MAM)

The Miracle of Laughing

Some days you just can't get much lower. Caregivers aren't the only people who experience these "bottomed-out" times, but piled on top of the daily load of caregiving, the impact of these times can be greater.

My lowest day as a caregiver happened when my grief over Art's death came face to face with the reality of caring for our four children alone. The funeral was over, friends and family gone. It was just me and the kids, grieving as our ages and personalities allowed. One son angry, the other quiet, one daughter demanding, the other mothering. And somehow I was still supposed to be the caregiver. Instead of changing IVs and cleaning bed sheets, I was supposed to give the sole direction, the only understanding, and single wise responses. How could I ever do it?

At the bottom of my adequacy well, my sister arrived. She'd planned it that way, saving her visit until everyone else had left. Within hours, the closeness we had shared in the past came flooding back. While the kids returned to school, she got me up and doing "projects." That's when we decided to install a closet organizer.

Things didn't go well. While she held one end, I'd try to fit and screw in the other. But nothing fit, and I never got the screws going in straight. My sister tried, but she wasn't much better. That's when our frustration turned into a joke. Every fumble we made, every board that slipped, every screw that refused to twist began to make us laugh. We laughed until the tears came. We laughed until we had to drop the organizer and run for the bathroom.

I laughed for the first time in weeks.

That laughter happened thirteen years ago, yet I remember it as if it were yesterday. It changed nothing, yet it changed everything. My kids were still grieving. I was still hurting, overwhelmed, and inadequate. But when I hugged my sister good-bye, I knew God had used her to give me a miracle. On the worst of my worst days, I'd remember that organizer and smile.

"A cheerful heart is good medicine, but a crushed spirit dries up the bones" (Prov. 17:22).

Lord, sometimes it's hard to laugh. Please come alongside caregivers reading this book and help them find their own miracle of laughing. (DH)

Questions

Sometimes my questions have no answers that I can find. However, sometimes the Lord uses me to answer other people's questions.

At the age of eighty, my stepfather, Al, came in sixth place in a bicycle race for riders over the age of fifty. He continued to ride his bike approximately fifty miles a day right up until age eighty-four, when he had a stroke. When I went down to Southern California to visit him and my mother, I hoped that something I'd learned over the years in taking care of my husband would help my mother.

As it turned out, the Lord was able to use me to help my stepfather. As we sat in his hospital room, Al kept asking why. Suddenly he stopped and apologized for questioning God. As I lifted up a brief prayer for something that would comfort Al, the Lord reminded me of all the times I'd asked questions and hadn't received any answers. God had used several psalms to help me learn to praise him without knowing the answers. In one of them, Psalm 10, David asks God all kinds of questions in the beginning, but by the end of the psalm, without his knowing any of the answers, his questions have turned to praise.

I reminded my stepfather of this. He smiled a lopsided grin and thanked me. Then he began to praise God even in the midst of his stroke. He had found the peace he searched for, and it remained with him until the Lord took him home a few weeks later.

It helps to remember we don't always need to know the answers. And yet, it's OK to ask God questions. God is still in control. He is there for us each step of the way. And, we may have the opportunity to take what we've learned and use it to help someone else who is going through times of caregiving. We will be blessed when we do.

> *"The sovereign Lord has given me an instructed tongue, to know the word that sustains the weary" (Isa. 50:4).*

Heavenly Father, help me to know that even when I don't have the answers, you do. Thank you. (MAM)

No Regrets

I've done a lot of things. I've raised four children, traveled around the United States, taught college, written books, and spoken publicly. Generally I continue to enjoy a full, active life. But of all my experiences, caregiving has left the deepest impact on me. When I chose to take care of my husband, it didn't just affect my life; it affected my heart.

I have incredible caregiving memories of tender moments and intense pain. I've seen death's reality cause a private-praying man to say, "Will you pray with me?" I've heard the warm, satisfying words, "I'm glad you brought me home." I've tasted a thousand tears and smelled their salty wetness. And I've felt the all but tangible arms of God holding me.

Back then, however, during the day-to-day load of caregiving, I only occasionally got glimpses of the richness being added to my life. So often I couldn't see past the six meals a day or the mental wall I put up to protect me from too many well-meaning comments. So often I could only cling to God and return to my favorite Psalm 27 verse about believing that I'd see God's goodness in the land of the living.

I'd repeat this verse on some of my darkest days, taking comfort from the promise. It was as if David knew how I felt, how I needed tangible goodness. I didn't know what it would look like, but I just wanted the hard days over and easier ones ahead. I couldn't grasp that the depth of feeling and living I was experiencing as a caregiver would touch every day of my future for good. From my empathy toward others to my view of God, I reaped incredible earthly good from my caregiving experience.

Today I'm a strong person with no regrets that I chose to give physical care to someone I loved. God used it to produce some of the best parts of who I am now. Knowing this has helped me see why God added one more verse after my one about seeing God's goodness in the land of the living.

> *"Wait on the Lord; be of good courage, and he shall strengthen your heart; wait, I say, on the Lord!"* (Ps. 27:14, NKJV).

Caregiving is so *today*, Lord. Often I can't even imagine what it will bring to my future. But keep me waiting on you. Keep my courage strong. (DH)

Sinkholes

Recently on the news, I heard about a house that suddenly had a basement that wasn't there the day before. It had been caused by a sinkhole. I smiled as one of my kids asked what we would do if our house sank, and then I told her we've survived several sinkholes over the last few years.

The first one I remember is when the doctor told me Lee probably had Alzheimer's disease. Then came Lee's decision to move to Oregon. Lee had always wanted to move to Oregon after he retired. Each fall we had visited his sister there, and I loved Oregon—but move there now? I didn't want that sinkhole. After all, all my friends and support were in Southern California. I needed to stay there.

Another sinkhole was making the decision to put Lee into a nursing home. I'd told myself over the years that I wouldn't do so until the doctor told me I had to. However, the doctor wasn't going to decide for me. This was one decision I had to make on my own.

The time came when Lee not only had to be watched twenty-four hours a day, but he became incontinent. Three of the children refused to stay home with him. That left two who were willing to give me a break. If Selena wanted to go someplace, however, John couldn't. He had to stay at home and watch his father. If John had plans, then Selena was stuck at home. The hole kept getting deeper and deeper. The only way for my last two teens to have any type of normal life was for me to put their dad into a nursing home.

Often when I pray about a decision at night, I wake up in the morning with the peace I need about the decision. God sent me that peace again when I needed it—after praying I woke up knowing it was now time to put Lee in a nursing home

I hope you will remember each time you encounter a sinkhole that you can grab onto God and his promises and let him pull you out, just as he has done for me.

> *"Be content with such things as you have. For he himself has said, 'I will never leave you nor forsake you'"* (Heb.13:5, NKJV).

Thank you, Father. You have pulled me away from the hole each time I have come close to falling in. (MAM)

Take Joy

Fra Giovanni, a Christian who had his own difficult times, wrote, "The gloom of the world is but a shadow; behind it, yet within our reach, is joy. Take joy." What a challenging, awesome statement! Can one choose to reach out and take hold of joy, just as a child takes an ice cream cone from her father? I thought joy just happened and certainly not at my request.

During the years of caring for my parents and grieving for them, I noticed that often in other areas of my life some joyous things were happening—gifts from God I had not sought. At the time, it seemed paradoxical that joy could find a place in my heart right beside grief, but it did. If God gives joy without our seeking, can I also seek joy, by choice reach out and take joy?

My answer to Fra Giovanni's challenge came when I read an account about a Russian nun who had been arrested by the Communists. They sent her to a labor camp in Siberia. Guards there decided to make her denounce her faith. When she would not, they stood her outside in the arctic winter with no coat, cap, boots, or gloves. They laughed at her. "Let your God keep you warm!" They expected her to beg to come in soon and renounce her faith. She did not, so they left her there to freeze.

Darkness fell around the nun. Knowing she would die, she praised God, rejoicing that she would soon be in heaven with her Lord.

In the morning the guards saw her still standing in an attitude of prayer where they had left her. It must have been that she was frozen to the ground and so stiff she hadn't fallen over. They marched out to dispose of the body, but, to their amazement, she was alive and praying. This was only the first shock. When they took hold of her, she felt as warm as if she'd been in a heated room all night. She had been utterly untouched by the cold. Needless to say, many prisoners and some of the guards ceased to be atheists that day.

Now, when I think of taking joy, I think of that nun. I think she chose to take joy. She reached out to Christ and rejoiced in the truth that death is the beginning of a life so wonderful that God could not keep still about it; he had to send Jesus to tell us and show the Way.

In Christ we have so many privileges. So much joy is available to us that many of us never reach out to take. Can we know and love him as well as that faithful nun? Can we dwell in him as trustingly as she did? If we can, I firmly believe he will fill us with joy, despite the pain that comes from living in this world.

There is so much more to life than our present sufferings. As much as life hurts right now, we can believe this one thing: God wants to give us joy to take with the pain.

"We are God's children. . . . co-heirs with Christ, if indeed we share in his sufferings in order that we may also share in his glory. I consider that our present sufferings are not worth comparing with the glory that will be revealed in us" (Rom. 8:16-18).

Heavenly Father, I don't always know how to reach out to you. Thank you for reaching out to me. Help me to see what is real and joyous beyond my sorrow and suffering. Help me to take joy! (EL)

Appendix I—Caring for Yourself

Here are some things that worked for us:

- Read the Bible daily.
- When you wake up, say good morning to God.
- Start a thanksgiving journal. Every night list three things from that day for which you are thankful.
- Every day keep an appointment with God to listen for him in a devotional quiet time.
- Keep physically fit by incorporating simple exercises into your daily activities. Examples: Do sit-ups and ham string stretches in the bath tub. Tighten abdominal and buttock muscles by repeated contractions while driving the car. Jog in place while watching TV or listening to music.
- If daycare is available, take your loved one regularly to daycare.
- If you have a computer and modem, get online for helpful caregiver information, networking, and emotional support.
- For peace of mind, carry a pager whenever you leave your loved one with someone else.
- Get lost in a book for fifteen minutes.
- Step outside once a day to see, feel, and hear God's creation: wind, rain, sun, snow, grass, flowers, trees, birds.
- Wear your watch upside down to remind yourself each time you look at it that Jesus is with you right now, right where you are.

- Wear your watch on the opposite arm to remind yourself to resist a stressful attitude you wish to change.
- Buy yourself a blossoming potted plant.
- If you have good health, thank God and enjoy it. You cannot take your loved one's place by feeling guilty.
- Talk to God all the time about everything.
- Treasure your friends, and let them know your prayer needs.
- If you can't get to church, ask church to come to you: Listen to the taped service. Let your pastor know your needs. Let a visitation committee know you need a visit.
- Dig in the dirt. Plant seeds or seedlings in the ground or window box or planter or pot.
- If your church has a support group for caregivers, join it. If it doesn't, can you start one, even if it is only contact by telephone?
- Locate an educational support group for people who are dealing with the disease or disability that your loved one suffers.
- Recall and treasure the good times. If you have photos in boxes, label them, and put the best into memory albums.
- Begin to learn something you've always wanted to do.
- Always eat well—a good breakfast and a balanced diet, adequate protein and plenty of vegetables and fruit.
- Give your regrets to God. Write them down; read them over to him; ask him to turn them into his good purpose; give them to him; and light a match to the list.
- In the fall, plant spring bulbs in a pot so they will bloom in the house in the middle of winter.

- Set up a bird feeder near a window where you and your loved one can both see the birds.
- Go to your doctor and dentist for routine checkups.
- Lie down to rest once a day. Relax your muscles, one by one, starting with toes and ending with tongue and throat. When you learn to be utterly still and relaxed, you will no longer feel the pressure of the bed under you.
- Learn other relaxation exercises and regularly practice them.
- Learn about nutritional supplements and take what your health allows.
- When depressed by grief, do the next normal thing, whether it be brushing teeth or taking out the garbage. Take the next normal step and then the next.

Appendix II—Resources for Caregivers

Publications

Magazines:

Exceptional Parent: Parenting Your Child with a Disability, P.O. Box 3000, Dept EP, Denville, NJ 07834

Today's Caregiver, P.O. Box 800616, Miami, FL 33180-8616

Books:

Callanan, Maggie and Patricia Kelley. *Final Gifts.* New York: Poseidon, 1992. Cases of "near death awareness" written by hospice nurses.

Fish, Sharon. *Alzheimer's: Caring for Your Loved One, Caring for Yourself.* Wheaton, IL: Harold Shaw, 1990.

Harwell, Amy. *Ready to Live, Prepared to Die: A Provocative Guide to the Rest of Your Life.* Wheaton, IL: Harold Shaw, 1995.

Hayden, Edwin V. *Beloved Sufferer.* Boston: Standard Publishing, 1987. How one man copes with his wife's disabling illness.

Mace, Nancy L. and Peter V. Rabins. *Thirty-Six Hour Day: A Family Guide to Caring for Persons with Alzheimer's Disease and Related Memory Loss Diseases.* Baltimore: Johns Hopkins University, 1982.

McKenna, David L. *When Our Parents Need Us Most. Loving Care in the Aging Years.* Wheaton, IL: Harold Shaw, 1994.

Meyer, Maria M. with Paula Derr, R.N. *The Comfort of Home: An Illustrated Step-by-Step Guide for Caregivers.* Portland: CareTrust Publications LLC, 1998. Filled with practical nursing helps for caring for the ill and the disabled at home.

Roach, Marion. *Another Name for Madness: One Family's Struggle.* New York: Simon and Schuster, 1986.

Rushford, Patricia H. *Caring for Your Elderly Parents: The Help, Hope, and Cope Book.* Grand Rapids: Fleming H. Revell, 1993.

Strong, Maggie. *Mainstay.* Chester, NJ: Bradford Book, 1997.

Tepper, Lynn M. and John A. Toner. *Respite Care Programs.* Philadelphia: Charles Press, 1993.

Upton, Rosemary. *Glimpses of Grace: A Family's Struggles with Alzheimer's Disease.* Grand Rapids: Baker, 1990.

Watt, Jill and Ann Calder. *Taking Care: A Self-Help Guide for Coping with an Elderly or Chronically Ill or Disabled Relative.* Vancouver, BC: Self Counsel Press, 1986.

Online Sites for Caregivers:

There is a wealth of online information and help for caregivers. Just place these words in your search program: *disabilities caregiver support.* Or look up the following specific sites:

Care Support Groups. Set up to give peer support. *http://www.uhs.berkley.edu/FacStaff/CARE/CAREGroups.html*

Caregiver Assistance Network. Located in Cincinnati, OH.

Sponsored by the Catholic Church. Provides links to many caregiver resources. *http://www. archdiocese-cinti.org/carenetw*

Family Caregiver's Support Network. Located in Toronto, involved with technical supports for caregivers. *http://www3.sym patico.ca/fcsn*

Family Caregiving Options. Guides and directories for caring for the aged by the Department of Health and Human Services. *http: //www.aoa.dhhs.gov/aoa/webres/f amily.htm*l

Today's Caregiver **online.** The magazine mentioned above. *http: //caregiver.com*

Useful Addresses and Phone Numbers:

Many of the following organizations have newsletters available to the public.

Children of Aging Parents
2761 Trenton Rd.
Levittown, PA 19056
(215) 945-19056

National Alzheimer's Disease and Related Disorders Association
70 East Lake St.
Chicago, IL 60601
(800) 621-0379
(312) 853-3060

National Family Caregivers Association
9621 E. Bexhill Dr.
Kensington, MD 20895-3104
(310) 942-6430

National Hospice Organization
1901 North Ford Myer Dr., Ste. 902
Arlington, VA 22209
(703) 243-5900

National Organization on Disability
910 16th St. NW, Ste. 600
Washington, D.C. 20006
(800) 695-0285

Stroke Club International
805 12th St.
Galveston, TX 77550
(403) 762-1022

Places to Call for Information:

AIDS Information Hotline,
1-800-342-2437

American Council for the Blind,
1-800-424-8668

American Diabetes Association,
1-800-232-3472

American Kidney Fund,
1-800-638-8299

Association for Retarded Citizens,
1-800-433-5255

American Cancer Society,
1-800-227-2345

AT&T Special Needs Center,
1-800-233-1222

Cystic Fibrosis Foundation,
1-800-344-4823

Disability Information & Referral
Service, 1-800-255-3477

International Shriners Association,
1-800-237-5055

Juvenile Diabetes Foundation,
1-800-223-1138

National Association for Sickle
Cell Disease, 1-800-421-8453

National Easter Seal Society,
1-800-221-6827

National Easter Seal Society,
1-800-526-3456

Spina Bifida Hotline,
1-800-621-3141

United Cerebral Palsy,
1-800-872-1827